BY OX TEAM TO CALIFORNIA

To my sister, Charlotte Dunning Baker,
whose constant nagging induced me to undertake
the writing of my memories of my life across the plains.

INTRODUCTORY.

When my two great, stalwart grandsons were little shavers, it was their favorite habit in the early hours of the morning to come creeping into bed with grandmother. Their soft little arms would twine lovingly about my neck and kisses from their dewy lips were pressed upon my cheek and brow. And were I ever so far away in slumber land their sweet voices clamoring for a story would banish all sleep from my drowsy eyelids. Usually they selected their own stories from the numbers I had so often repeated, but invariably wound up, when I had exhausted my fund, by saying, "Now, grandmother, tell us about crossing the plains."

The true stories appealed more strongly to them than all the illusory conceptions of fancy, from the fact, perhaps, that I could relate what really had occurred better than I could draw from my imagination. Be that as it may, they never wearied of hearing how I crossed the plains, climbed the Rocky mountains and traveled many months on my way to California. To gratify them and their dear mother I have consented to write up for them the history of my overland journey.

Those who may favor the succeeding pages with their perusal must not expect any attempt at fine writing, or glowing descriptions. The author's intention is to furnish a plain, unvarnished tale of actual occurrences and facts relating to her long journey. Nothing not strictly true will be admitted into its pages, and if some of the incidents related be found of a thrilling character the reader will experience satisfaction in knowing that they are not the results of imaginary picturing. Whenever a personal adventure is narrated, it will be found to illustrate some particular phase of character, and none are recounted which do not convey information.

As I recall those years after the lapse of time, they are as vivid as the memory of yesterday's events. It has been a positive delight in the midst of this modern life, to live over some of those scenes. Those peculiar conditions no longer exist, for the advent of the overland railway and the customs and usages of more civilized life have done away with much of the fascinations of romance and adventure.

If I have not laid sufficient emphasis on the difficulties and discouragement which we encountered, it is not because there were not numerous obstacles to overcome, but in turning the mind upon the past, the more pleasant memories stand out in bolder relief; even when the cares and responsibilities weighed most heavily upon us, we had that saving grace of humor which enabled us to meet situations otherwise insuperable, and to gather courage whereby we might endure them all.

Necessarily in recounting these events so closely identified with our life on the plains this narrative has assumed an autobiographical character to a larger extent than the author could wish, and I humbly beg pardon of the reader if I have exceeded the canons of good taste.

All through that tedious and extended time I kept a journal of every day's happenings as they occurred, but after our arrival in California we settled on a remote ranch, and in those early and primitive days, books, magazines or literature of any kind were rare among the farming community where we were located. My journal proving interesting to our neighbors, was loaned and re-loaned from one family to another until at last it fell into the hands of some careless persons who allowed it to be partially destroyed, particularly that part relating to the first months of our journey. Many names of rivers, streams and different points and places have slipped from my memory, but the principal places and events of our journey were so strongly impressed upon my then young mind, that they have become indelible and time can not efface them. Perhaps the repetition of them over and over to my little grandsons and their young playmates served to strengthen them in my memory, and, while I may be lacking in ability to embellish this humble history I can still give the plain facts and incidents of that never to be forgotten journey.

CHAPTER I.

IT WAS in the fall and winter of eighteen fifty-nine that my husband and I decided to emigrate to the far West. Imprudent speculations and other misfortunes had embarrassed us financially to such an extent that our prospects for the future looked dark and forbidding; we then determined to use the small remnant of our fortune to provide a suitable outfit for a lengthy journey toward the setting sun. We were both young and inexperienced, my husband still in his twenties, and I a young and immature girl scarce twenty years of age. I had been raised south of "Mason's and Dixon's line." My parents were well-to-do Southern people, and I had hitherto led the indolent life of the ordinary Southern girl. My husband, educated for a profession, knew nothing of manual labor, and had no idea of any other vocation outside of his profession; nor had he the training to make a living on the plains of the West, or the crossing of the continent in an ox team a successful venture. However, we had youth in our favor, and an indomitable will to succeed, and I have since learned by experience that a kind providence watches over fools and children. Since that long ago time when I look back at the temerity of our undertaking I have wondered why, and how, our older and wiser friends permitted us to be turned loose upon the wilds of the West without a guardian. We were two such precious dunces, but with a most exalted ego, and the utmost confidence in our ability to brave the dangers of the undertaking.

A journey across the plains of the West was considered a great event in those early days. It was long thought of and planned seriously with and among the various members of the family to which the would-be traveler belonged. Whoever had the temerity to propose turning their backs on civilized life and their faces toward the far-off Rocky mountains were supposed to be daring with a boldness bordering on recklessness.

Emigration then meant the facing of unknown dangers in a half-savage country.

After many lengthy debates over the manner of transportation, and a diversified quantity of advice from our numerous friends, as to the merits of horses, mules or oxen, we at last decided (and it proved to be a wise decision) to purchase three yoke of strong, sturdy oxen and a large well-built emigrant wagon; roomy enough to hold all we wanted to take with us, and in which we might travel with some degree of comfort. In due time the oxen were bought. The six animals were young and had never been broken, to the yoke. When they were driven to our home, turned loose in our barnyard, they were as formidable a lot of wild brutes as the eye ever gazed upon, as agile as deer, and as handy with their heels as with their horns. Not one of us was brave enough to venture into the corral with them, and we soon realized that we had six white elephants on our hands. Finally my husband found a negro man who agreed to break them to yoke and chain. It proved to be rare sport to our neighbors watching them in, the somewhat difficult task of training that bunch of young steers. But with time and patience they became more amenable to yoke and chain, and sullenly submitted to be attached and to draw the wagon. I shall never forget the first time I ventured to ride behind them, we had invited some of our neighbors who were brave enough to risk their necks to ride with us. There were several ladies and children and a man or two included. It was our intention to drive our new team a short distance into the country and give our friends a foretaste of what a journey would be behind the slow-moving cattle, but before we had driven a block our skittish and newly-broken team took it into their heads to run away down the hilly streets of our village, pell-mell, first on one side of the street then the other. In vain my husband called "Whoa, Buck, whoa, Jill" to the leaders. It only seemed to add to their fury, and as they recklessly sped along in their blind rage, the way proper matrons and prudish maids climbed and scrambled out of the rear end of that wagon was a sight to behold if not to describe. After repeated trials and much patience on our part, our wild oxen became tractable, and long before the end of our journey we had become very much attached to them, and they in turn had learned to love us, becoming docile and kind as kittens, any one of them would follow me wherever I led, eat out of our hands, or allow me or our little son to ride on his back.

The strong wagon with which we had provided ourselves had a staunch canvass covering, made water tight and firm enough to defy the ravages of wind and storm. Then came the loading and packing of provisions, raiment, and all the other paraphernalia necessary for a long trip. What to take and what to leave behind us was the problem that confronted us every day. Many times was the wagon loaded and unloaded before it proved satisfactory. Many of our most cherished treasures had to be left behind to give place to the more necessary articles.

The report of fabulous mines just discovered in the Rocky mountains had extended far and near, and the Pike's Peak excitement was then at fever heat It was at this time that thousands of people had set their faces westward towards that mecca of their hopes. While our friends imagined that we, too, would make that point the end of our pilgrimage, yet we had decided and promised each other that if Pike's Peak and its environments did not come up to our expectations we would push on to California. With that final objective point in view we provided ourselves with provisions sufficient to last us for six months or even longer.

Young as I was at that time we had been married nearly five years. We had a dear little fair-haired son, Robert, who was the pride and joy of our hearts. I began at once to prepare an outfit for both him and myself which I thought suitable to wear on the plains. In this I showed the callow ideas of an immature mind which would not be guided by older and wiser heads — proving also that my conception of roughing it for six months was very primitive. Among the other necessary garments in my outfit I had made two blue cloth traveling dresses with an array of white collars and cuffs. When a sensible elderly neighbor suggested home-spun or linsey woolsey as being far more appropriate, I scorned her advice. These fabrics were worn only by the negroes in the South. I assured her that I intended to look as neatly and well-dressed on the plains as at home. However, I soon discarded my cloth gowns and my collars and cuffs, as I will relate farther on.

When our plans were fully matured and all our arrangements nearly completed for an early departure there was revealed to me a most startling discovery that in the course of a few months the stork intended to make us another visit. Welcome as he might have been under more favorable circumstances, his promised coming in the near future brought consternation to our hearts, and we were afraid our plans would all have to be changed. We feared the perils of our journey might prove to be too hard for me to endure under these new circumstances. But I was well, young and strong; had the courage and bravery of ignorance, besides, we hoped to reach the end of our destination and find a home and resting place before the final advent of the stork's promised visit, which I was careful to conceal from my friends. I did not wish to give my dear parents any unnecessary worry; they were already filled with dread and anxiety at the undertaking we had so lightly assumed. We concluded to make the best of what could not be helped, and with stout hearts still continued our final preparations.

Everything being now in readiness, we waited impatiently for the warm days of spring, as we were to depend mostly on the wild grass of the prairie for food for our stock which now consisted of the aforesaid three yoke of oxen, a full blooded Arabian saddle horse and a milk cow.

It was the third day of April, 1860, that my husband and eldest brother, Sam, who accompanied us as far as Pike's Peak, left the little town of Hannibal, on the Mississippi river, and started overland across the state of Missouri for St. Joseph, where by rail and train myself and little son joined them. We remained in St. Joseph a day or two to make my farewell visit to my dear sister who resided there.

On the fourteenth day of April we left St. Joseph, driving aboard the ferry for the farther shore of the muddy Missouri river, accompanied by my sister, her husband and a few other friends. We landed in a little village on the Kansas shore, and drove our friends out a few miles on the prairie, and made our first halt for our noon-day meal in which our friends were to join us for the last time. It was a sorrowful picnic, for our parting hour was near at hand.

Seven and forty years ago it was a serious thing to say good-bye to all that was nearest and dearest, to uproot ourselves from home and go forth into the wilderness into many and unknown dangers.

My sister and friends were to return by the ferry to St. Joseph. My husband and brother were too tender-hearted to remain and witness our sad parting. They hurriedly gathered the cattle from where they were feeding on the short grass, yoked them to the wagon, put my little son into the wagon beside them and drove slowly away, leaving me to bid my friends a long and last farewell.

I never recall that sad parting from my dear sister on the plains of Kansas without the tears flowing fast and free. Even now as I write, although so many long years have passed since then, I cannot restrain them. We were the eldest of a large family and the bond of affection and love that existed between us was strong indeed. It was like tearing our heart strings asunder. But such sorrows are to be endured not described. As she with the other friends turned to leave me for the ferry which was to take them back to home and civilization, I stood alone on that wild prairie. Looking westward I saw my husband driving slowly over the plain; turning my face once more to the east, my dear sister's footsteps were fast widening the distance between us. For the time I knew not which way to go, nor whom to follow. But in a few moments I rallied my forces, and waiving a last adieu to my beloved sister, turned my dim and tear-stained eyes westward and soon overtook the slowly moving oxen, who were bearing my husband and child over the green prairie. Climbing into the wagon beside them, with everything we possessed piled high behind us, we turned our faces toward the land of golden promise, that lay far beyond the Rocky mountains. Little idea had I of the hardships, the perils, the deprivation awaiting me. When the reality proved to be more than my most vivid imagination had pictured it, I was still able to endure it with a staunch heart, but often as I walked ahead of the team and alone, thoughts of home and my dear father and mother would almost overwhelm me with grief. As each step bore me farther from them, the unbidden tears would flow in spite of my brave resolve to be the courageous and valiant frontierswoman. I had been taught that a wife owed her first duty to her husband, and hard as it seemed I had the courage to do what I had promised under the highest and most solemn sanction.

We had been several days on our journey before I began to realize the immolation and sacrifice I was to endure; giving up my comfortable home and all my dear ones, cut off from the congenial society of my associates and personal friends, the ease, luxuries and comforts of civilized life. Enduring the disagreeable drudgery of camp work, the constant exposure to the elements, the glare of the scorching sun, the furious and fearful thunder storms that so often overtook us, the high winds, and blinding, pitiless sand storms that blew for days without cessation, the dread that settled down upon us at nightfall for fear of wild beasts and the other dangers that so often menaced us in our utter loneliness, the necessity of still moving onward, each day, whether we were in the humor for traveling or not. At first the novelty attending the starting out on such a trip and the continuous change of our environment kept up our interest. But as the days wore on the irksome monotony of the journey began to pall upon me, and I spent many unhappy hours which I tried to conceal within my own breast, sometimes confiding to my journal my woes and disappointments, but managed to keep up a cheerful exterior before my husband and brother. Gradually, however, I became used to the peculiar situations by which I was surrounded and learned by daily experience how to surmount the trials and difficulties, and with a naturally cheerful and optimistic temperament soon became philosophical enough to take things as I found them and make the best of the situation.

CHAPTER II.

Camping In Kansas— A Novice With Camp
Fires —Marching On Foot.

Our first night in camp was near a small stream. On the banks were a few stunted and wind-blown trees. The forage for our stock was not good. During the night the cattle strayed from camp in search of better grazing, or the inclination for the old pastures, and turned backwards toward home. When morning dawned we had nothing left but our "Arabian steed," which fortunately we had securely picketed, or he too, might have deserted us. James, my husband, took the horse and went back rapidly over the road we had traveled the day before. My brother, taking the field-glasses, went on foot in another direction to find traces of our wandering herd. With my little son I was left alone in camp to wrestle with the campfire and breakfast.

I must admit that my first experience with real cooking was on this journey. Like many other Southern girls I had learned how to make a delicate cake or a fancy pudding, but never before had I tried to cook a meal. You can well imagine what a difficult task it must have been for me to build a campfire, get my kettle to stand upright on the rolling wood, keep the smoke out of my eyes and ashes out of the food, hampered as I was with my blue cloth traveling dress and the great effort required to keep my white cuffs clean. A short distance from our camp an old man and his two sons had set up their tent. I learned that they also were en route for Pike's Peak, coming from their thrice remote New England home. I was conscious that they were watching my poor efforts very closely, and after I had upset my coffee pot, and the camp kettle had turned over and put out the little fire I had at last got started, the elderly man came to my assistance, rebuilt my fire, adjusted my kettle in the proper way, expressed his kindly sympathy in our dilemma, and then bidding me a polite good day returned to his own camp. As the morning advanced my Yankee neighbors soon did up their camp work, folded their tent, and moved along on their way, leaving me alone on that forlorn prairie, with not a soul in sight anywhere. Had I been a timid creature I might have wailed my lonely plight. My little son and I ate our poorly cooked and joyless breakfast alone, after waiting long for the return of my husband and brother. Not until the noonday sun was high in the heavens were my tired and strained eyes gladdened by the sight of them afar off driving the lost cattle before them. After that experience the stock was herded until bed time, and then securely staked to prevent another occurrence of that kind.

I very soon discarded the blue cloth dress and white collars and cuffs, fully realizing that they were not just the proper thing for camp life. Fortunately I had with me some short wash dresses which I immediately donned, tied my much-betrimmed straw hat up in the wagon, put on my big shaker sun-bonnet and my heavy buckskin gloves, and looked the ideal emigrant woman. The first days of such a journey, however commonplace, were interesting to us. Every faculty was on the alert. Even so trivial a thing as a jack-rabbit rising out of the grass, scared, and scampering with long leaps, striving to widen the distance between us, was able to hold our attention. Or we watched the misfortunes of a fellow traveler by the wayside, who, in his great haste, had neglected to lubricate his running gear properly; hence a hot-box which he was vainly trying to cool off with a wet blanket. Crossing a deep stream on whose opposite side were a few rough houses and the usual saloon, the entire population turned out to see us drive through the village. As we passed the last house, an old crone was bending over her tub busily washing, but she stopped her labors long enough to ask us in drawling tones, "be you gwine to Pike's Peak?" Answering her in the affirmative, we inquired the name of the village we were just leaving. "Oh," she replied, "this is Mason City." Anywhere through Kansas three or four log huts constituted a city.

My young brother who traveled with us was a youth of susceptible proclivities, fresh from the restraints of college life, and with the exhilaration of his new found freedom unusually elated. For was not his face turned towards the wonderful land of the Golden West? While we were yet children around the home fire-side, we had planned a life of travel and adventure, and now our childish longings were to be realized. He had an absorbing passion for nature, for every curious formation of rock or stone, a quick eye for all the beauties of the unfolding landscape, a ready ear, too, for every touch of humor, and was hilarious over the interminable picnic that he imagined we had begin. Nature had also endowed him with a nimble tongue, and he was constantly telling us funny stories of college life. Often we would laughingly accuse him of drawing the long bow, on relating some very unusual experience. In vain we would try to outwit him and play our own jokes upon him, but his lively retorts were nearly always to our complete discomfiture. Generous hearted boy was he, and round the camp fires and over many of the wearisome stretches of our journey he made the hours seem shorter with his cheerful badinage.

Part of my work when in camp was cooking. I have already acknowledged my great deficiency in that accomplishment. The bread-making at first was a total failure. When I attempted to make light rolls for breakfast they were leaden. My husband, wise man that he was, ate them in silence, but my humorous brother, less polite, called them sinkers. I felt chagrined at my failure, but persisting in my efforts I soon overcame the mysteries of the dried yeast cakes with which I had been supplied, and in a short time learned to make sweet and wholesome light bread.

As we had no tent we slept in the wagon, my brother taking the rear end for his "Pullman," spreading his blankets above the bales and boxes, never seeming to mind the ridges and uneven surface of his couch. James, myself and our little son, occupied the front of the wagon. We had a huge old-fashioned feather bed, that made sleeping above the boxes and barrels a trifle more comfortable. During the day it was necessary to stow away the beds more compactly to enable us to get at the stores beneath them. This also was my work while the men brushed and curried the stock, lubricated the wheels of the wagon, and reloaded the various camp equipage. James was kindly solicitous for the welfare of his cattle, giving the oxen the same careful grooming that our horse received, and they fared much better for this attention, looking sleek and fine for the extra care.

When I had finished my part of the camp work I would wrap myself in a warm shawl and start out on the road ahead of the team. The early spring mornings were keen and cold and I felt the need of brisk exercise. I had always been an enthusiastic pedestrian and greatly enjoyed walking over the gently undulating plains of Kansas. It was our endeavor to make from twenty to thirty-five miles' progress westward every day. If the weather permitted and the roads were not too heavy from the frequent rains, it was my habit to walk the entire distance. As I grew accustomed to the continued exercise, I could accomplish the long walk with ease. At other times, mounting my horse, I would enjoy a gallop over the prairies, occasionally getting a bad fall. My horse was a kind and gentle animal; but I soon discovered that he was possessed of one most treacherous fault, namely, when frightened instead of swaying or shieing sidewise, he would suddenly squat, and the best rider would become unseated. I had been thrown from his back once or twice in this manner, luckily without injury, and Sam, my brother, made great sport of my failure to stay in the saddle on these occasions. This mortified me exceedingly, as from my early childhood I had ridden horseback. There were few horses that I dared not mount, and I was extremely vain of my skill as an equestrienne. However, one fine day, he too, came to grief. I had been riding for several hours and becoming weary dismounted. My brother vaulted lightly on the horse and rode swiftly away. While I stood admiring his graceful pose and the fearless manner in which he rode, suddenly I saw him go flying out of the saddle and quickly strike the ground, and not on his feet either. After his own failure, he ceased to vex me with his jests and raillery.

We had only been a few days out on our journey when we witnessed an electrical storm, something unusual at this time of the year. This storm was frightful in the extreme for us as we were so unprotected from its fury. The sky was overcast with dark and threatening clouds, a low sullen murmur as of distant wind filled the air. The lightning blamed incessantly as it lit up the darkening horizon. The thunder burst forth in peal after peal of deafening reverberation. We hurriedly drove our frightened team into camp as this storm continued. By midnight a furious gale swept over the bare prairie. Our wagon, exposed to the fury of the wind, shook and rocked in such a manner, that every moment we feared it would be overturned. Yet with all this flurry of the elements scarcely a drop of rain fell in our vicinity. Farther on we discovered next day by the condition of the roads there must have been heavy showers. For the first two or three weeks it rained almost daily, which made the conditions very uncomfortable and with difficulty we made our fires from the water soaked wood and cooked our meals under the falling rain.

When the days were bright and clear the travel through Kansas was delightful. The aspect of the prairies in the early morning sunshine was most alluring. The air was fresh and bracing, filled with the fragrance of countless spring flowers, and every little blade of grass hung with drops of dew that scintillated like jewels as they waved in the gentle breeze of morning. The sweet note of the meadow lark was music to the listening ear. On every side was high waving grass that covered these vast stretches of undulating land. I rode or walked over the tufted plain, seeing, unvexed by sound of wheel or human voice the pleasant sights along the way. The solitude upon this wide expanse of open plain was absolute. No smoke arose in the clear air from any habitation. No cattle browsed upon the succulent grasses. No whistling plowboy tore the sod-grown turf with his shining plow, nor uprooted the tinted blue star flower that sprang up on every hand. There were numerous winding streams fringed here and there with miniature forests. Our cattle grew sleek and fat with the nourishing food nature so lavishly provided. And just within the woodland that fringed the banks of some small stream, we would halt for the night, happy to find both wood and waiter, the two great essentials for a comfortable camp.

When we had been two weeks or more on the road we came to one of the largest streams in Kansas, the Big Blue, timbered with sycamores, cottonwood, oaks and occasional elms. After breakfast one morning, my brother loaded his gun and took a short excursion in search of prairie hens. We had seen numbers of them along the road. Much to his great disappointment and ours also, he was unable to start a single one in the high grass. This we learned was the fate of most huntsmen at this hour of the morning and season of the year. These birds wait until the sun gets high and warm before they come forth from their hiding places to strut and coquette with each other. This led Sam to take a much longer detour than he had anticipated and it was nearly noon before he presented himself wet and bedraggled, but triumphantly bearing one prairie hen. Only wounded by his shot, it had weakly flown just beyond his reach, until it led him near the shelving banks of the Big Blue, when in a last successful effort to reach his fluttering victim he had stepped too near the edge of the crumbling banks of the river, and huntsman and bird disappeared beneath the waters of the stream. Luckily grasping a willow sapling as he went down and still holding on to his feathered victim, he pulled himself on shore and came back to camp elated with his adventure. We enjoyed the flavor of the wild bird, as our appetites had palled on salt meat. Up to this time wild game had been scarce near the road. As we proceeded prairie chickens, quail and the ringdove became more plentiful and proved a grateful addition to our larder.

Here and there along our way we saw numerous dugouts which we were told were occupied by herdsmen. These were supposed to be a secure shelter from the cyclones that came so suddenly upon these vast plains which were treeless; and as lumber was scarce they also afforded cheap homes for the pioneer emigrants who occasionally settled here. Anything that looked like a home attracted us and brought to our minds the association of home life from which we were going farther and farther away.

While we were camping on the Big Blue, we were in the midst of a large company, who like ourselves, were bound for Pike's Peak. The beautiful undulating meadow lands were dotted here and there with tents. The blue smoke from numerous camp fires arose on all sides, while huge prairie schooners were anchored within hailing distance; in many instances like our own serving for tent and shelter. Cattle were leisurely feeding on the luxuriant grass, campers were fishing or hunting along the stream, while the women were on duties bent or sitting by their camp fires. The children of the emigrants, released from the strain of travel, were romping over bush and briar, and their shouts of glee resounded as some unfortunate stubbed his brown, uncovered toes and fell face forward on the soft earth.

As we approached Nebraska, the country became wild and somewhat more sterile. All signs of human habitation disappeared entirely, and with them the wild game became less abundant. No longer the prairie hen or the quail flew from the grass as we approached, though plovers and doves still seemed plentiful.

Between Big Sandy and the Little Blue river was a monotonous drive, hot and uncomfortable, with only a few cottonwoods to enliven the landscape. Here we found a settler whose humble, but comfortable cabin was filled with children of all ages; they seemed to overflow from doors and windows; their brown and sun-burned faces forming a strange contrast to their tow white hair. We were invited to visit them in their humble home and were surprised to find so much culture and marks of refinement in this far away land. The mother was an educated eastern woman, and in spite of the hard work necessary on a new farm and the encumbrance of a large and growing family, she, without the assistance of either maid or servant performed all the labors of her household, and still found time to instruct her children in the rudiments of a good education. Her courtesy and good manners I never saw excelled in the best society. While the cabin was very meagerly furnished, yet on the cheap wooden shelves that adorned the walls were many good books of standard authors, which bore the marks of being well read. The children were clean and well clad although their clothing did not need the services of a French laundry; neither did the mother have time to dawdle away her time at bridge or go to card clubs, even if these things had existed or been thought of in that isolated home on the plains of Nebraska. The father was a typical sturdy rancher, both horseman and herdsman, with a rich vein of humor combined with strong common sense. He proved to be most interesting, amusing and instructive. His fund of back-woods stories and his inexhaustible humor kept us in a constant roar of laughter. We left these cheerful people with feelings of regret.

CHAPTER III.

TO THE inexperienced traveler the approach of nightfall is hailed with joy, for the camp fire is among the chief pleasures of out-door life. We vied with each other in replenishing its cheerful blaze. There was always a fascination in watching it kindle from its little glimmering light into the roaring flame. The flicker and glow illuminating the countenance of those nearest the fire for a brief moment, bringing out every feature with a peculiar distinctness and just as suddenly obliterating them with an intense shadow. Then, too, if the night was bleak and the wind blew his frosty breath, you were reminded by your freezing back that picturesqueness and comfort did not always go together. The brilliant tongues of flame and the innumerable sparks floating off into the air, had no charms for those who were roasted on one side and frozen on the other. The flying sparks on windy nights would blister any exposed surface of the skin, while the smoke with every change of the breeze was whirled into your eyes. For all that, in many of our lonely halting places, the bright and cheerful glow of the camp fire served to drive away the gloom that surrounded us, and keep the wolf and howling coyote at a respectful distance. When we were far out on the great plains, with no wood or tree in sight, our main dependence for any sort of fire was on the despised buffalo chips. These emitted scarcely any flame, and we hurriedly cooked our evening meal before its unsatisfactory glow dissolved into a few light ashes. Then we appreciated fully, in spite of its minor drawbacks, our bright wood camp fire.

In the early stages of our journey before we had grown wise by experience, it had been our custom when we came to a stream at evening to camp before crossing it. Storms that occurred so frequently at night caused these streams to rise suddenly and overflow their banks. These shallow brooklets which we could wade easily at night, would become angry, rushing torrents before morning, filled with drift wood and debris. While these floods were raging, we had no alternative but to swim our cattle across or wait for the stream to subside. We had made this mistake once too often and at last found ourselves, as the rain continued, waiting in camp for several days for the waters to fall. But we were not alone. Each day brought us more company and before the water had subsided there were fifty or sixty other emigrant wagons in view, their tents dotting the landscape on all sides, while their stock was grazing on the rolling prairie around us. The emigrants worked about their camps, the women busily employed in cooking or in trying to dry their clothing that had been drenched by the continual rain. Sitting around their wagons were other unkempt, soiled and bedraggled women, most of them lean, angular and homely, nearly every one of them chewing on a short stick, which they occasionally withdrew and swabbed around in a box containing some black powder, while a muddy stream oozed from the corners of their polluted mouths. It was evident to the most casual observer that they were snuff dippers from Arkansas or Tennessee.

A number of ragged and half-clothed children of both sexes swarmed around their camp, bare-footed and bare-legged. One of the women, to whom my attention was particularly called, sat disconsolately apart from all the others, who were pottering around their camp work or gossiping in little groups. Her thin knees were clasped by her bonier hands, and her towsled head drooped forward. There was a most tragic expression on her care-worn countenance and she looked as if she cared for nothing on earth. A strong measure of human suffering was depicted on her hopeless face, and it seemed as if nothing would rouse her. But in this I was much mistaken. Two of her bare-footed boys had committed some childish prank which roused the fierce anger of one of the men who stood idly by smoking his short pipe. In a voice thick with sudden rage he called the boys to him. The terror and the panic depicted on their faces plainly showed their great fear and instead of obeying the surly call they started to run. The man, seizing an ox goad, soon overtook them, and quickly applying it to their naked legs caused them to emit screams of anguish with the severity of the blows. Then in another instant I saw that mother aroused from her seeming apathy. With one bound, like an enraged tigress, she cleared the wagon, catching up a horse whip as she ran, and soon reached the man, who was so unmercifully beating her children. Her attack was so sudden that he was unprepared for the onslaught. She rained quick and sturdy blows on his head, face, arms, anywhere in her blind fury. It required the combined efforts of two men of the company to make her desist. The man whom she had beaten was wild to chastise her in return, but those who had separated the angry couple protected the woman. The boys in the meantime had scampered out of sight. After many hot words, a truce was declared and the commotion soon died down. I comforted myself with the thought that we were not obliged to travel with such an inharmonious company.

We were now being continually overtaken by numerous trains of the faster horse and mule teams, many of them bearing on their painted wagon covers such fanciful legends as "Pike's Peak or Bust," "Root Hog or Die." Long before our slow moving oxen reached Denver, we met those same teams coming back, and underneath their legends was the brief word "Busted" or "The Hog's Dead." The wild rush was not confined to wagons alone. Hundreds of men had pack animals which were loaded with blankets, provisions, coffee pots and frying pans. A few even had hand carts which they pushed with their light outfit before them. Traveling alone with our one wagon, independent of the numerous caravans that overtook us, we were passed by most of them, for our oxen were much slower than the horse and mule teams, which seemed to predominate. Yet the days were full of excitement, as we came into contact with such a diversified lot of human nature. Nearly every state in the union was represented, all looking forward with eager eyes toward the rich mines of the Rocky mountains.

These vast prairies of Kansas and Nebraska were sadly deficient in bridges. While at low water many of the streams were not difficult to cross, yet often we found ourselves at the brink of others whose steep and slippery banks looked very formidable. Down the precipitous incline the wagon would seem almost to topple over on the oxen, then into the deep stream and up the difficult pull on the opposite side. We had been on the road nearly a month, owing to the delays of wet weather and the high water we encountered, when we came to a large stream too deep and treacherous to ford, called the Republican river, where arrangement was provided to cross by a rope ferry. At this place we found a large number of families, with an immense herd of horses and cattle, migrating from Illinois and Missouri to California by the way of Fort Kearney, where they would strike the old military road. They had been trying to swim their stock over this stream. This was slow and difficult and their patience was well nigh exhausted. It was impossible to get such a large number of animals ferried over in a hurry. Consequently we had to wait our turn and nearly two days went by before we could take this primitive ferry across the deep stream.

One often hears the plains of the West spoken of as monotonous levels. But here and there they rise and fall in gentle undulations, sometimes crossed by narrow streams fringed by the homely and ragged Cottonwood. One morning, while climbing a rather high divide, we caught sight of our first antelope, and my impulsive brother wanted to give them a chase at once; but they soon showed us by their swift flight that they had no desire for a closer acquaintance with us. We were sadly disappointed, for by this time we were beginning to grow tired of bacon and salt pork, and longed for a taste of fresh meat. In a day or two they became more frequent and less wary, and one afternoon we sighted several in a group so intently feeding that my brother laid one of the beautiful creatures low with his rifle. The others soon sped out of range. They were beautiful, graceful creatures; in color a yellowish brown on the upper portions of the body and almost white on the under parts. The nose, horns and hoofs were black, with eyes bright and most beautifully expressive. We afterwards saw numbers of them in the distance, but this was the only one we ever came near enough to shoot. I could not forget the startled look in the beautiful eyes of the timid creature as it fell to the ground wounded and dying, and I did not relish the meat prepared from it as I had anticipated.

One Sunday while resting in camp, my husband accompanied me and our son to a small stream some distance from our wagon, where we could take a refreshing dip in the clear water. We had enjoyed our bath greatly. Leaving the middle of the stream I seated myself on its banks and as I was drawing forth my foot from its depths, a huge snake came gliding out of the water close by my side. With true feminine instinct I uttered a shrill scream and started on a swift run toward camp in my scanty bathing attire. Before my husband could overtake me, however, I had recovered from my fright and went back for the remainder of my clothing. Frequently when walking the sight of a huge rattler would cause me to make a sudden jump into the air to avoid coming in contact with the repulsive creature. James, who ever kept a watchful eye on me as I walked ahead of the team, would jokingly ask, "Why did you jump so high and run so swiftly at intervals?" These reptiles were quite numerous on our route, rattlesnakes predominating, with many others not so venomous, but just as repulsive.

CHAPTER IV.

Buffalo Country—Returning Gold Seekers—
Our Whiskey Barrel

BY THE frequency of the trails that continually crossed our road, we found we were nearing the land of the buffalo. Now and then the heads and skeletons of buffaloes dotted the plains, and in certain localities the ground was fairly white with the bleached bones. We never imagined that any use could be made of them, but many years after that time I was informed that a regular trade had sprung up for these bones, and that a number of Eastern firms did a large business in shipping them to their markets, where they were used in manufacturing buttons or ground into a fertilizer. As yet we had not seen a herd of buffaloes. We had listened to many tales of how they loped over the plains, coming swiftly with bended heads, tearing the turf in their mad rush, which no obstacle could oppose. They had been known to run directly through and over trains of emigrant wagons leaving scarcely a vestige, and while we were now constantly on the lookout for a sight of these animals, it was with fear and trembling.

One morning we had just finished our breakfast of salt pork, fried mush and coffee, of which I had partaken with little relish. My hitherto pampered appetite had begun to rebel at the coarse and homely fare. I was hungry for some fresh meat. Nearly a quarter of a mile beyond us was another camp of emigrants, men, women and children, with their full complement of tents and wagons. Suddenly from this camp I saw a man come running toward us, and as he came nearer, pointing and gesticulating madly, I heard him shouting "buffaloes." Looking quickly in the direction he was pointing, I saw a large herd of a hundred or more. They seemed to be making a wild dash for our camp, bellowing, as they ran with lowered heads in a long awkward gallop. Several of the men were running on foot to get a shot at them. My brother leveled his Sharp's rifle and fired, but it seemed rather to hasten than arrest their flight. On they came with rapid strides, and crossed the stream almost beside our camp. One shaggy headed old fellow, shambling up the bank, was tired at several times by a number of the men just as he entered the water. Falling to the ground as he emerged on the bank near our side, he caused the rest of the shaggy herd to veer suddenly in their course, taking their way between the two camps, and quickly disappeared around a group of low rolling mounds just beyond us. My little boy and myself had taken refuge in the wagon, expecting every moment to feel the trampling of their hoofs, for we had heard much of their rushing through and over trains in their mad flight, leaving them wrecked and their occupants mangled beyond recognition. The buffalo the marksmen had wounded so that he could no longer follow the herd was quickly dispatched. The men dressed the carcass, and each one of the campers took a portion of the animal. When we received our share I immediately raked together the coals and embers of my breakfast fire, and broiled thereon a piece of the fresh meat to satisfy my craving appetite. It proved a great disappointment, for it was tough, strong and dry. I had heard that no meat could equal or excel that of the buffalo, but the piece I had cooked was not relished. I also learned that this was the meat of an old bull, and we had not even taken the best part of the animal, which was the hump on the shoulders and was considered a very choice morsel. After this we saw many large droves of buffaloes in the distance. There must have been thousands, but they had grown wary. The overland traffic in 1860 was so enormous that the buffaloes kept too far from the main traveled road to give much sport to the skillful hunters. We never again fired a shot at one. Occasionally we were able to buy from the Indians a few pounds of what was then termed "jerked buffalo." This was strips of the wild meat dried in the sun and wind without salt. The tongues of the animals dried in this manner were fairly palatable, but one could chew for hours on one small piece of the dried meat, and the longer you chewed the bigger it grew. However it was a change from salt pork and bacon.

We passed hundreds of new-made graves on this part of our route. One would imagine that an epidemic had broken out among those preceding us, so frequent were these tell-tale mounds of earth. One day we overtook a belated team on its way to one of the distant forts with only a man and his wife. The wife was quite ill in the little tent, having given birth to a child a day or two before, which lived only a day. The father had put it in a rude box and laid it away in its tiny grave by the wayside. The poor mother was grieving her heart out at leaving it behind on the lonely plain with only a rude stone to mark its resting place.

I think it must have been near the middle or last of May when we met our first Indians, a band of thirty or forty Cheyennes. They did not trouble us to any great extent, although we felt rather annoyed at their proximity. The first Saturday after we came into the neighborhood of this tribe we called an early halt in the afternoon. For several days the grazing for our stock had been very poor, but in this Indian country the buffalo grass was more plentiful, and while it was short yet it stood very thickly over the ground. The roots of this buffalo grass were long and sweet, and the cattle devoured them, with as much relish as the tops of the grass. In all stages of ripeness it was very nutritious, and the stock throve upon it. Taking advantage of this good pasturage we concluded to wait over a day or two and let our cattle recruit, while James made some needed repairs to the wagon. It gave me a convenient time to do my necessary washing and baking. Continual moving on did not give much extra time for cooking, and bacon, beans and bread, day after day, became monotonous; so I gladly embraced this opportunity to have a change of diet. I made dried-apple pies with bacon drippings for shortening; and some ginger cookies, with the same ingredient entering largely into their composition in place of butter. The latter was a scarce commodity, as all that we had was from the milk of our one little cow. We had soon discovered that by pouring our morning's milk into a covered can in the wagon, the continual jolting would churn it as we moved along, and at night we would have butter enough for our evening meal if we used it very sparingly. For breakfast our bread was dipped in gravy as usual! These two days in camp near a stream gave us an opportunity for a bath, and me a chance to wash the alkali dust from my hair, and to do the necessary mending of our clothing.

We were now in the midst of numerous bands of roving Indians, not hostile to us, but intent on begging or stealing. Whenever or wherever we made our camp they soon found us and never left us throughout the day. This Sunday I had discarded an old, worn-out hoop-skirt that I had worn thus far on my journey, and much to my amusement and amazement as well, it was immediately donned by a huge Indian brave, who strutted proudly among the group of Indians who were squatting around our camp. As the skeleton hoop composed the larger part of his attire he was a sight to behold. Even the stolid squaws were provoked to mirth at the ludicrous spectacle.

The following Monday found us ready to move on, and we began very soon to meet team after team of disappointed "Pike's Peakers" returning East. We talked with a number of them who had not even gone so far, but had been assured by many returning that the whole country was a vast humbug. They, too, had lost courage and faith and were going back to their homes. They told us of hundreds in Denver who would gladly work for their board, that men who were in the mines could not average a dollar a day, and all who could get away were leaving, urging us to go no farther. But we were not to be intimidated by their doleful tales. We would see for ourselves and continued on our way.

On the level lands and river bottoms of Kansas and Colorado were countless numbers of prairie dogs. These harmless little animals lived in villages, which we traveled through for weeks. These marmots made the air lively with their chattering, a peculiar short shrill squeak, rather than a bark, and the honeycombed soil was in motion with their antics. Sitting on their haunches on top of their pinnacled earth-burrows, they would peer curiously at us with their shining, beady eyes, until our approach jarred on their nerves, when they would suddenly disappear into the depths of their burrows. In many places there would be hundreds of them on an acre of ground. Beside the prairie dogs the coyote became familiar with us, never by day at close range however, but at nightfall he could be heard prowling about our pans and kettles.

Occasionally we passed a small settlement where a hardy pioneer had built for himself a rude home, partly and sometimes wholly of sod, with a rude forge and a primitive blacksmith shop and the inevitable whiskey mill. As we went farther west these little settlements were called cities, although consisting only of wretched little mud cabins, a few acres of land plowed but unfenced, and sometimes beside these cabins a wayside house, from whose portals swung a wooden sign bearing the name Tavern. They were queer structures, partly tent and partly cabin. A few rough posts would be driven into the ground. These supported a ridgepole, across which some old pieces of canvas and ragged sailcloth formed a rude and primitive shelter, large enough, however to hold several barrels of whiskey. On a dusty shelf above a counter made of boards resting on two empty barrels were a number of broken and cracked glasses, some half-emptied bottles, a few cans of oysters and sardines, and this constituted the entire outfit of the so-called "Tavern." Probably the Boniface of this crude establishment knew his business better than we did and had decided not to squander his capital in articles that were not considered a prime necessity.

And here I found as well as at other places on the road that whiskey was considered a prime necessity of every outfit on the plains. This had been the subject of many spirited discussions between my husband, brother and myself before and after starting on our trip. While laying in the supplies for our journey, every one said we must take a barrel of that article with us. In spite of strenuous objections on my part, which were overruled, the whiskey was bought and duly stored with the rest of our provisions. At different points on our journey I began to notice when we camped at night and also at our noon halt that our wagon had a drawing attraction for many of the other emigrants whose camps were in the vicinity, and it finally dawned on me that the barrel of whiskey was the alluring charm. While my husband was a temperate man, yet he was socially and hospitably inclined, and many of the emigrants, taking undue advantage of these qualities, would too frequently for their own good and my peace of mind visit our camp. I knew it was useless to complain or interfere. But I patiently bided my time, and one day when no one was around, I quietly loosened the bung of the barrel of whiskey and by nightfall there was nothing left of the precious stuff, save the empty barrel and the aroma of its spilled contents. Not even a bottle was saved for emergencies and we never needed it.

The continual walking day after day over the hot, dry roads, the wading through heavy sand and dust for much of the distance, caused extreme suffering to the feet of many emigrants. My husband had not taken into consideration that he needed larger and roomier boots for this long tramp and continued to wear the same size he had been accustomed to wear at home. After a few weeks he began to complain that his feet hurt him. Every morning it required greater effort to get on his boots. At length, finding his feet continued to enlarge, he tried splitting his boots open to give his feet more room. This of course let in sand and alkali dust, which irritated them still more. There was no store of any kind on the road where we could buy either boots or shoes or any other merchandise. Finally his feet became so painful that he discarded boots altogether, and becoming too disabled to walk, was compelled to ride in the wagon for several days to allow the painful swelling to subside. My brother and I took turns in driving the oxen. Finally we met a band of Indians from whom we were able to buy some moccasins made from deer skin, which were large, soft, and comfortable, and afforded great relief. They proved to be strong and durable, and lasted until we reached Denver, where he was able to replenish his foot-gear in larger proportions.

CHAPTER V.

Indians

We gradually approached more desolate regions where we could look for miles over immense distances and see nothing but the long, dim perspective, and yet no sooner were we settled in our camp at evening and our fire lighted, when our Indian friends would appear, fathers, and mothers, and, judging from their appearance of old age, grandfathers and grandmothers, besides children of all ages, squatting as was their custom on the ground, watching silently though with greedy hungry eyes every mouthful that was cooked or eaten, sitting so near my fire that I was compelled to step over their feet in getting to and from the mess box while I prepared my evening meal.

By many crude efforts in the sign language and an earnest use of a few Indian words that we had picked up among them, we attempted to carry on a sort of "Pigeon English" with the various tribes with whom we came in contact. There were two words we found that were thoroughly understood by them, and universally used wherever we met them, and they were "Bishket" and "Coffee." It would have been impossible for us to have fed any number of them, but frequently I gave an old man or old woman a cup of coffee and a biscuit, which they greedily swallowed, or a lump of sugar to a child, which was seized with extreme avidity. After finishing our own meal and scraping off the remnants of food, bones, and meat rinds from our plates to the ground, there would be a mad rush of every Indian for the refuse, and it was amusing to see the scramble that would ensue for the discarded scraps. After lingering a while and finding there was no prospect of getting anything more to eat, they would slip away one by one as silently as they came, but there was no sign of any habitation, unless they burrowed in the ground.

When camping one Sunday near the Platte river we were surrounded by Indians as usual whenever we stopped for any length of time, and their continual attendance left us little, privacy. This Sunday I had washed my long hair to free it from the dust of travel and was engaged in brushing and combing out the tangles, having near me a small hand mirror. One brave who had been watching me very intently, was such a hideous looking creature that I wondered if he could know how repulsive he looked. Without a moment's thought I took up the hand-glass and held it before him. I never saw such a look of surprise and consternation as came over his stolid countenance. He took the mirror in his hand, looked intently into it for some moment's turned it over, examined and looked again. Then taking it among the other Indians who were loitering in our camp, he showed them the mirror with their different reflections therein, which seemed to cause them much curious amusement, I think this must have been their first experience in seeing themselves as others saw them. After a while he brought the mirror back to me. I had given up all hopes of having it in my possession again. At length this Indian with several of his tribe silently departed, but in a few hours returned with some new recruits, all decked in their paint, feathers, beads, and blankets. Approaching me he made signs for the mirror again. When I handed it to him he burst forth in a guttural sort of laugh and immediately turned it on his new followers, who in turn expressed much amazement at this first view of themselves. The Indians generally were not voluble, but a wonderful flow of unintelligible sounds came to my ears as they discussed among themselves the merits or demerits of the strange little mirror.

A band of mounted Sioux met us one day. They were friendly in their advances and stopped to trade with us. I would state here that the Sioux Indians were the finest looking warriors we had seen. Their ponies and horses were richly caparisoned, and their blankets, which were supplied by the United States government, were gay with bright colors. The headdress of the men was unique and imposing. Sable braids of hair fell down each side of their painted faces, and the crowns of their heads were decorated with the colored feathers from the wild birds of the mountain and plain. Their buckskin jackets were jeweled with beads and hung with the teeth of wild animals. Descending from their long braids of hair, were graduating discs of bright silver made from the half-dollars that were paid them by the government. These were hammered out very thin, until the first was as large as a small saucer, and the others grew gradually smaller as they reached nearly to the ground. These discs were hung on strong but slender strips of buckskin, and glittered gaily in the bright sunlight, as the warriors, mounted on their fleet ponies galloped over the plain.

We found the Sioux tribe very friendly, too friendly in fact, for my peace of mind, for one huge brave, gayly bedecked and most grotesquely painted, took a great fancy to me. Bringing a number of ponies to our camp, he at length made my husband understand that he wanted me in exchange. This was the first time I was really frightened at their advances. Though I knew they were a friendly band and under the care and protection of the government, yet I was filled with a fear that I could not wholly overcome, and urged my husband to move on as rapidly as possible, so we left our camp next morning before the break of day. About noon, as we ascended some low rolling hills, I looked back on the plain and saw a number of mounted Indians approaching us very rapidly and driving a large band of ponies before them. My heart almost ceased beating, as we were completely at their mercy if they meant us harm. Finally they overtook us. We halted our team and had a lengthy parley with them. They proved to be the brave and his followers of the day before. He had added more ponies to his band, thinking my husband had refused to trade because they had not offered a sufficient number. After numerous signs and shakes of the head, they at last understood there was no prospect of business. Very reluctantly they mounted their ponies and left us, to my great relief. The next few days I rode very closely in the wagon. Before they departed, however, I cooked them a good dinner, and James treated them liberally to his best tobacco, so we parted good friends.

Early in the forenoon of one eventful day we met the first war-like band of Indians. I was walking some distance ahead of the wagon, when in that clear bright atmosphere there appeared on the level plain a cloud of dust far off to the left of our road. I usually carried the field glasses with me and I quickly looked to see what I could discover. At first the dust was so dense that the eye could not penetrate it, but soon there was revealed the forms of many moving animals. My first thoughts were "buffaloes," and I hurriedly retraced my steps to the wagon and the protection of my husband and brother. I had scarcely reached the wagon before my ears were filled with the din of most uncanny character, and out of the cloud of dust on numerous ponies rode a formidable looking band of Indians, many of them arrayed in the most whimsical and barbarous style that one could imagine.

There was not the slightest attempt at uniformity in costume. Some of them wore the discarded and ragged clothes of emigrants, from which hung strings of buckskin knotted with gay beads and buttons, and interspersed here and there with a tin spoon or fork stolen from the emigrants. Their faces were painted in the most grotesque manner, and their coarse and matted hair, which grew long and scraggy, was ornamented with tufts of feathers from the wild birds of the plain and the tails of wild animals. Some were attired in the usual breech cloth, while many were wrapped in gaudy blankets of red and blue. Among this motley crowd were several that might have been devils let loose from the so-called infernal regions, for on their beetle brows were crowns made from buffalo horns, their limbs naked to the knee, were covered with buckskin leggings and on their feet were moccasins. Others had made great effort to array themselves in fanciful attire of skins peculiarly painted and embroidered by their skillful squaws. Yet we discovered among the number some few who were not dressed at all.

As they bore down on us in their rapid approach we were almost speechless with fright. Our first impression was that we were to be annihilated at once. We saw at a glance that they were warriors ready for the fray, and had made elaborate preparations to go forth on the war path. They were armed with all sorts of weapons, knives and shields of various and strange devices, but the bow and arrow, the natural weapon of the red man was most in evidence. They surrounded our wagon on all sides, making numerous signs and gestures and uttering words of Indian jargon that were Greek to us, for we could not understand a syllable. Then despairing of making themselves understood, they pointed first east then west, then to their ponies and held up their hands with extended fingers. All in vain. We could only shake our heads. At last, finding it was only a waste of time to parley with us, their chieftain gave the command, and re-mounting their ponies, they sped away, giving voice again to their blood-curdling yells and leaving us to recover slowly from our suspense. We drew a long breath of relief when we realized that we were still possessed of our usual amount of hair. We afterwards learned that they were in pursuit of some other marauding band of Indians who had stolen and run off with a large number of their ponies.

That night we camped near a few cottonwoods on the banks of a small stream. The wind blew in fitful gusts and the limbs of the cottonwoods rocked restlessly, making mournful sounds. From every side we were startled by noises we could not place; strange rustlings caused us to peer sharply into the shadows, footsteps seemed to stealthily approach and then skulk away; even the thin and scraggy bushes appeared to suddenly close together as if some one were behind them, and we feared that the Indians of the day, knowing that we were alone, might surround us in the hours of darkness, take us unawares, and massacre us. None of us slept through the long hours of that night. We were afraid to close our eyes for fear of their stealthy return, but dawn found us unmolested.

I have said that neither the Indians nor ourselves could understand each other in conversation. Yet we found on several occasions, that they had picked up and readily adopted a number of phrases from the emigrants, particularly the teamsters, whose vocabulary of profane words was extensive. The usual salutation of the Indians whom we first met was "How." But after hearing the irate teamsters from day to day cursing their overworked and often contrary cattle, the Indians very quickly adopted some of their pet phrases. Often when we met them they saluted us in this manner, "Gee, Whoa, Haw. G-d d-n you," and did not appear to know that this was not the regular manner of saluting.

We saw but few Indian lodges. Those we did see were of the Sioux and Pawnee tribes. Usually their camps were remote from the traveled highway. We had been induced to take a shorter cut that took us in sight of one of their encampments. These lodges were built in circular form, a number of light poles forming the support, around which were stretched buffalo hides which the squaws had ingeniously sewed together. Some of these lodges were unique in their way, decorated and painted in accordance with the red man's idea of art, with grotesque faces and queer figures of animals, and strange hieroglyphics emblematic of something in their creed. Many of these tribes did not bury their dead. Perceiving at some distance poles set upright on the ground and what appeared to us like a huge shelf above them, we saw on approaching nearer the form of a human body well wrapped in blankets and buffalo skins, and found that it was the Indian manner of burial.

A little familiarity with these aborigines will convince one that it needs a very poetic mind to make them even bearable. We found them not only lazy but covered with vermin and while squatting around our camp it was the principal relaxation of the squaws to spend their time overlooking the heads of their papooses and catching and killing the insects that inhabited them, very much to my disgust. The Indian man abhors labor, and they looked on the white man with scorn and derision whenever they performed any duties to relieve the labors of their wives. The squaw accepted her life of toil as her just due for being born a woman. It was the squaw who dressed and tanned the skins and made the garments that the lazy Indian wore. It was she who manufactured the rough utensils in which the food was cooked. It was she who took down and pitched the rude wigwam and gathered the fuel, dressed and cooked the game, often walking for miles to bring it home, when her arrogant lord returned from the hunt. She made his rude tents after tanning and dressing the rough hides of which they were made, his moccasins and his clothing. In many of the tribes these women were exceedingly skillful, and it was wonderful what an amount of work they could accomplish with the most primitive tools. In addition to all this, when she felt the pangs of approaching motherhood, the squaw would betake herself to the banks of some nearby stream and there all alone without the aid of a nurse or accoucheur her babe would come into the world. After giving her new-born child a hasty dip in the cold stream, it was wrapped in a rough skin, strapped to a board and borne back to camp on the mother's shoulders. Then with all the stoicism for which the Indian character is noted, she resumed her interrupted duties.

CHAPTER VI

Trials Of The Spirit —Thirsting For Water—
Gathering Buffalo Chips—Sick On The Desert
—Bay Rum, Bergamont, And Castor Oil—
Mirage

Even to the most courageous there were hours of depression and discouragement. Our days were not always sunshine, nor our route through pleasant lands. The fertile soil covered but a small portion of our journey between the Missouri river and Denver. After the first month or six weeks of our pilgrimage the change of vegetation became very apparent. The sage brush, that forerunner of sterile soil, began to crop out here and there. The farther we traveled the thicker it grew, particularly in the dry and sandy localities. Its only redeeming feature that I could discover was that it served for fuel in the absence of any other wood. We were amazed at the magnitude of these barren, unfenced plains. The occasional little hamlet was left behind and only at rare intervals did we come on the solitary cabin of some brave pre-emptor, who showed more courage than wisdom in settling on such a forlorn hope in Uncle Sam's domains. The wind had full sweep over these barren plains. Many times it was almost impossible for any one to walk against it. Frequently we staked our wagon down with ropes and also our stock to keep them from stampeding, for the wind and showers of blinding sand came with such force that neither man nor beast could face it. At such times we could cook no food, but crawling into the wagon, tying down the covers on every side, were forced to content ourselves with dry crackers and molasses.

These winds tried my patience sorely and seemed to act directly on the nerves; and as for cooking around a camp-fire when the wind was blowing a gale, it required a greater amount of fortitude and self-control than I possessed. I tried to keep my hasty temper within bounds, but no matter on which side of the fire I stood when cooking, the ever shifting smoke blinded me, and the gale whisked my short skirts over the fire, until I found not only my clothes but my temper ablaze. I would make a brave effort to be cheerful and patient until the camp work was done. Then starting out ahead of the team and my men folks, when I thought I had gone beyond hearing distance, I would throw myself down on the unfriendly desert and give away like a child to sobs and tears, wishing myself back home with my friends and chiding myself for consenting to take this wild-goose chase. But after a good cry I would feel relieved, and long before I was again visible to husband or brother, I had assumed a more cheerful frame of mind, whether I felt it or not.

Besides wind and rain storms we would often encounter great swarms of gnats, which would annoy our stock almost to the verge of madness, stinging our own faces and hands, getting into our food and making it impossible to drink our coffee, without first skimming them off. These swarms of insects would last two or three days before we would leave them behind us.

As we proceeded on our journey the streams of water grew smaller and farther apart and the great plains drier and dustier. There were days of travel with scarcely enough water for our stock, and that so strongly impregnated with alkali that a very small quantity would satisfy. Oh, how we longed for the sight of a cold, clear spring of water. We could sometimes see for miles ahead of us what looked to our longing eyes a lake of limpid water, but on coming nearer it we found it was only a thin alkali incrustation covering many acres of the smooth sands, and later on we were compelled to make a drive of nearly sixty miles without a drop of water for our stock. Our poor cattle were choked and dry with the great thirst. When at last they scented water they were almost unmanageable, and struck a bee-line for it, paying not the slightest attention to the roadway, but speeding as fast as they could travel over hills and hummocks, caring naught for the safety or comfort of those riding in the wagon. While in this almost arid region we endeavored to keep our small keg filled with water, but found it impossible to carry enough for our stock. Indeed we had to use it very sparingly ourselves.

Through many parts of Kansas, Nebraska, and Colorado the question of fuel was constantly before us. Days and days passed without seeing a piece of timber as big as one's little finger. Our only fuel was buffalo chips. This was the sun-dried excrement of that animal. It was my custom in the early hours of the afternoon as I walked, to carry a basket or sack, and fill it with buffalo chips, often wandering a distance from the road to find a sufficient quantity with which to cook our evening meal and enough to bake our bread for the next day. This proved at last to be quite a laborious task for me, because the numerous caravans ahead of us had gathered up all that lay near the roadway and I was compelled to cover considerable territory before finding a sufficient supply. The sack of buffalo chips became a heavy burden before I reached the wagon. I had been performing this task for days, when one afternoon we passed some low hills on which grew a few dwarfed and stunted pine trees. They were only about a quarter of a mile from the road, and I asked James and my brother to drive to them, and cut me enough of the wood to last us for a day or two. But men on the plains I had found were not so accommodating nor so ready to serve or wait upon women as they were in more civilized communities. Driving a lot of wayward cattle all day in the hot sun, over heavy roads of sand and dust was not conducive to politeness or accommodation. When the drivers were weary and foot-sore, they were none too ready to deviate a hand's breadth from the traveled road. Therefore, as it required almost half a mile of extra effort to get that wood for me, they thought it unnecessary trouble and refused.

I was feeling somewhat under the weather and unusually tired, and crawling into the wagon told them if they wanted fuel for the evening meal they could get it themselves and cook the meal also, and laying my head down on a pillow, I cried myself to sleep. When I awakened, I found that we had camped and they were taking me at my word. The only fuel in sight was across the deep and cold stream of the Platte, but they waded across the stream hatchet in hand, the water coming up to their hips. On the farther side grew some small willows which they cut and bore on their shoulders back to camp, and after many efforts at last got the fire to burn and the supper cooked. James came to the wagon where I was lying and meekly asked how much baking powder to put in the biscuits. I replied shortly, "Oh, as much as you please." I will admit that his biscuits that night were as light and nice as any that I have ever eaten, and both he and my brother were quite elated with their success in getting the evening meal, and said it did not matter whether I cooked any more for them as they could do just as well if not better than I did. The coffee also was fine, but the dried corn which they had tried to cook was not a complete success. This was a delicacy we did not indulge in every day. It was usually saved for a special treat for our Sunday dinner, and I had always put it to soak for several hours to soften it before cooking, a precaution the new cooks had not taken.

I was hungry and ate too heartily of the underdone corn. The consequence was that I was very ill with a severe and painful attack of dysentery for several days. Finally becoming so weakened that I could no longer climb in or out of the wagon, I was compelled to keep my bed as we journeyed along. The jolting motion of the wagon soon became a perfect torture to me, and at last became so unendurable that I implored my husband to take me out, make my bed on the sand and let me die in peace.

He, poor man, was very much alarmed at my condition, and was at his wit's end to know what to do for me. Complying with my wish, he had halted the team in the middle of the forenoon and was preparing my bed on the ground. We were in the meantime overtaken by another emigrant team, whose sole occupant was a blunt, old Missourian. He stopped to inquire the cause of our delay so early in the day. James told him of my illness, describing my symptoms. The old man then said, "What your woman needs is a good, big dose of castor ile. That'll straighten her out all right."

Now one of the most peculiar oversights in preparing for this journey was that we had not provided ourselves with any medicine. Not one of us had ever been ill, nor had we been accustomed to illness in our families, and our friends believing in the hydropathic treatment, had not suggested such a need to us. We were also five hundred miles from a drug store, but after a moment's thought, I remembered that among the toilet articles in my trunk was a bottle containing castor oil, bergamont, and bay rum, put up specially for a hair tonic that was much in vogue at that time. This was sought for at once by my husband, and pouring out a tea cup full of the vile stuff in order to get enough of the oil, with grim determination I swallowed it down. Oh, the horror of that draught! To this day I never smell the odors of bay rum or bergamont without the vision of a poor, sick emigrant woman lying on the sands of the desert. Offensive and obnoxious as the dose was, it had the desired effect and acted like a charm. I have since recommended the remedy a number of times. In a few days I was quite recovered and ready to continue our interrupted journey. I noticed that my men folks were only too willing to turn over the culinary department to me again, and really made quite commendable efforts to keep me supplied with fuel thereafter.

The United States government sent out many trains of provisions to the different posts that were stationed far out on the plains, and these wagon trains would often travel near each other for help and protection, their white canvas-covered wagons sometimes reaching as far as the eye could see. Many of these trains were composed entirely of ox teams, and their drivers had a profane vocabulary that sent cold chills over me. Never in my life had I heard such strings of oaths come from the mouth of man. These immense caravans were called bull trains and their captains called bull-train bosses. The men who drove the teams were called bull whackers. All of these government teamsters in their moments of leisure were anxious for something to read. Before leaving home I had stowed away among my belongings a few favorite volumes to while away the hours of enforced leisure: my Shakespeare, Byron, and Burns and a few others that I could not part with I soon learned to hide very carefully and peruse with drawn curtains, or they would have disappeared from my eye. The few novels and magazines that I possessed were loaned and re-loaned until they were so tattered and torn as to be scarcely legible. It was astonishing how great was the demand for something to read in those days of overland travel. The majority of those crossing the plains had taken no books with them, burdening themselves with nothing save the bare necessities of life. Anything in the shape of print was greedily devoured. Every scout, trapper, or other lone frontiersman with whom we came in contact would eagerly inquire for old newspapers, magazines or novels, — anything to read. It was impossible to buy reading matter on the road in those days. In fact over a stretch of five hundred miles there were only three or four post-offices, and from the time we left St. Joseph on the Missouri river until we reached Denver, three long months, we had had no news from home and the dear ones left behind us.

At intervals we were electrified with a passing glimpse of the overland stage, bearing the mails and sometimes passengers from the East, but they flew by us with such break-neck speed, that it was impossible to even hail them. Yet I still watched for them day by day for they seemed to be a connecting link between us and civilization. Occasionally we would pass an overland stage station, a low hut or cabin constructed wholly of adobe or dried mud. These huts were said to be very cool in summer and warm in winter, their walls being from two to three feet in thickness, and were considered proof against the severe blizzards that swept over the country, as well as bullet proof in attacks from hostile Indians. I often wished that I might look into one of those huts, but never chanced to pass one when the host was at home. I had not the temerity to invade one without invitation, although the latch-string invariably hung on the outside. We usually stopped only long enough to take a drink from the rusty cup that hung from a pail of water near the door.

One of the most wonderful sights on these desolate plains was the mirage. The first time this strange phenomenon appeared I was filled with astonishment. While riding one day along the monotonous level road and gazing ahead at the wide expanse of sand and sage brush, a peculiarly brilliant and dazzling light appeared like sunlight on the water. My first impression was that we were approaching a lake or some other large body of water. As I looked, this seemed to change, and a number of buildings came into view, but all upside down, and while still gazing at them they slowly faded from my vision, and the supposed water again came into view. I was so overcome with the wonderful vision that I could not wait for the others to overtake me, and turning my horse, rode rapidly back to the wagon to see if my husband and brother had witnessed the wonderful sight. They were as much surprised as myself, and though we had often read of the phenomena of mirages, this was our first sight of one. After that we saw them several times.

From Cottonwood after a tedious, long drive, we arrived one night at a place called Fremont springs, and here we found a fine spring of clear, cool, delicious water. For days we had climbed and descended hills and passed through a series of sand canyons. For many miles after leaving Cottonwood our road lay near the creeping, treacherous Platte. The Platte itself was not alkaline, but many times our trail was some distance from the river, and our cattle would become so thirsty before they could be driven to the river, that they would seek to satisfy their thirst in the many shallow lakelets that abounded near the stream, and these lakelets were in many instances almost saturated solutions of soda and potash. We ourselves as well as our poor cattle enjoyed the delicious draughts from Fremont springs, which was considered the finest water between the Rocky, mountains and the Missouri river. We felt like falling down and worshipping this fountain, cooling the parched lips of man and beast whose fate had led them beside the stagnant pool and dull, creeping, muddy waters of the Platte.

Much of our journey after leaving Cottonwood was near and in sight of the South Platte river, but its proximity failed to moisten the stretches of sand along our gloomy pathway. It crawled along between low banks, and one day I ventured to take a bath in its waters, but on descending its banks, the oozy loam glided too swiftly beneath my feet and in a moment I realized I was in its treacherous quick-sands. I scrambled up the bank by main force, shuddering to think how soon I might have been engulfed in the muddy depths of its deceptive waters. On these desert wastes the wind blew at a rate of ten knots an hour and it was so filled with sand that it seemed like earth in motion instead of air. Along this dreary route we walked day by day. Everything was grey. The few sickly weeds that grew upon its dry soil would crumble at the touch; here and there a single sunflower gave a touch of color; a few sickly cacti bloomed. Flowers that had enlivened the landscape farther back had entirely disappeared. In their place the naked land swarmed with ant-hills and myriads of grasshoppers and huge brown crickets abounded. At night the wind blew even more violently, and the tempest of sand that came flying with it filled the air, and everything that lay untouched for a time was powdered half an inch deep with it.

Through one of these storms the overland stage from the East overtook and passed us. It surged along bearing about a dozen wearied, dusty, dejected-looking passengers. I noticed that they seemed to be hanging on to life at the neck of sundry flat pocket flasks. As we came near Denver, the South Platte seemed to make its nearest approach to beauty, and in many places it was studded with beautiful islands, picturesque indeed with their emerald green foliage of graceful willows. When we neared Beaver creek a beautiful landscape began to unfold. The river seemed to widen out into a huge lagoon. I remember the rosy hues of a beautiful sunrise that unfolded to our view. The mirrored water was filled with wild ducks, the river swarming with teal and mallard, their beautiful green and blue plumage looking gay in the early sunlight as they glided through the water with exquisite grace.

The journey toward Denver might have been divided into four stages, — the prairies, the less fertile plains, the desert, and then the Rocky mountains. At this late day it is very easy to underrate the toilsome marches of many weeks — now that one can travel in forty-eight hours over an extent of country which forty or fifty years ago baffled the progress of the venturesome pioneer. I remember how joyfully we greeted the first scrubby pine trees, giving us hope that the desert was nearly past and the mountains were not far off. Their soft and tender green was soothing to our sunburnt vision, and when we halted at nightfall we found a numerous band, who had made the long journey through this woodless region, building huge fires with the dead pine branches, and taking solid comfort in the cheer and warmth of the ruddy, leaping blaze of which they had been so long deprived. Soon the foothills of the Rocky mountains were in evidence.

Arriving at Bijou, Colorado, we encountered one of the severest storms I ever saw on the plains. We imagined we had seen severe storms in Kansas, but this one descended on us so suddenly and the rain and sleet came down in such torrents, that we had scarcely time to stow away the provisions made for our evening meal. While James and my brother were hurriedly chaining our oxen to the wagon to prevent them from stampeding before the pelting rain and sleet, and staking the wagon to the ground to keep it from being overturned by the fierce wind, I and my little son climbed into the wagon for shelter. The noise of the rain and hail on our canvas cover was deafening and seemed as if it would tear our frail shelter into tatters. No warm supper for us that night. We crawled into our blankets damp, tired, and hungry, wondering how long it would continue. Not until after midnight was the wild fury of the storm somewhat abated. A drizzling rain succeeded which made the roads almost impassable for days, while the heavy grades became so steep and slippery that we were compelled to wait for help to pull us up their steep inclines. As we came nearer the foothills these high winds seemed to become more prevalent and swept over us at times with relentless force. Every night our wagon was securely staked to prevent an upset by the fury of the gale. These high winds no doubt accounted for the lack of timber, for the young trees were so rocked and wrenched that their roots were not firm enough to draw up what little nourishment the porous soil could give them.

But gradually a change was taking place. The pine trees which appeared at intervals, although stunted and dwarfed, gave variety and softness to the landscape which hitherto had been so monotonous and drear. The hills became more rolling, and the valleys deeper with water courses more frequent in their depths, and our thirsty stock could drink their fill without robbing those who came after us. The timberless plain ceased to be desert and was once more fertile. Our progress now was one of gradual ascent. In many instances our pathway was unlovely and unsatisfactory. Here and there a shady ridge forcibly reminded us of the drift of the many terrible sand storms we had so often passed through. When darkness came upon us, near some little mountain stream, where we made our lonely camp, our voices sounded singularly clear in the cool, clear air, and instinctively we drew nearer each other with the knowledge of our loneliness. This loudness of our voices was the first thing we noticed that gave evidence of a change of air from the plains. We could distinctly hear the sound of a human voice two or three hundred rods away.

Far out on the plains for miles before reaching Denver, we were told to keep a sharp lookout for a first view of Pike's Peak, and for many days we were straining our vision to the extreme limit. The first view I had of the mountain was in the form of a vaporous cloud. Gradually this began to form a sharper and more distinct outline, until at last we could see clearly the glittering peak, covered with snow, rising to a height far above all other peaks, like a sentinel watching over the plain. As our gaze rested from time to time on this Monarch of the Mountains, so full of majesty and power, other less lofty peaks were presented to our view, until finally the whole majestic range of the Rocky mountains was outlined before us. As our eyes were fixed upon the towering mountains looming up so grandly, we easily fancied that an ordinary swift pedestrian could reach them in a day's length. At any rate our slow-moving team would bring us to them in a few short hours. But for days our course westward still lay along the plain and over additional rising foothills, while many weary miles intervened before we entered these mountain gorges and explored the strange and mysterious paths leading us up and down through those lofty ranges.

CHAPTER VII.

Infant Denver—Hanging By The Vigilance Committee—An Indian And His Scalps—The Parting With My Brother—A Sale Of Glassware—On To California

At last in the latter part of June, after three months' wearisome journey, we made our way down the mountains and over the lower range of the foothills into the then primitive village of Denver. Picture if you can an almost level plain surrounded on all sides by towering mountains, whose highest peaks were snow crowned even in midsummer. In the center of this great plain stood Denver. I shall never forget our advent into that "City of the Mountain and Plain." A few days previous we had fallen in with several wagons with their full complement of men, women, and children, — a motley crowd, the men unshaven and unshorn, with long, sunburnt whiskers, their stained and weather-beaten garments begrimed with the dust and dirt of the plains, — the women and children with their huge sun bonnets pulled over sunburnt brows, ragged, unkempt and dirty, their short, rough dresses in tatters from coming into too frequent contact with the camp fire, many of them bare footed from the rough roads and long travel which had played sad havoc with their only pair of shoes. I doubt whether any one of us would have been recognized, so changed was our exterior from the trim and nattily-attired trio that left home in the early spring, now wearied with urging contrary and tired cattle over miles of treeless and waterless wastes, barren deserts and alkali plains.

I had pictured Denver a thriving, bustling, busy city, but nearly fifty years ago it was an exceedingly primitive town, consisting of numerous tents and numbers of rude and illy constructed cabins, with nearly as many rum shops and low saloons as cabins. Horses, cows, and hogs roamed at will over the greater part of the village. Very few of the humble homes were enclosed with a fence. These inferior shanties, built of logs and rough boards, were clustered together near the banks of Cherry creek. In the lower part of the town the vacant places were occupied by the Indian huts of a band of the Arapahoe tribe, who were at war with the Utes, and who trusted that the presence of the white man in their vicinity would afford protection to their families against attack, while their own braves were off fighting or stealing in the mountains beyond. The relations of the Arapahoes and the Ute Indians were not of the most cordial character, for hereditary feuds and occasional warlike sallies had from time to time disturbed that perfect mutual concord so important for neighbors to maintain. Each tribe prided itself on its superiority to the other, and it would be deemed a great disgrace for an Arapahoe maiden to marry a Ute, and vice versa. Their poor, overworked squaws were busily engaged in the labors of the camp, cooking their vile compounds, and making the skins of wild animals into the uncouth garments that they wore. Loafing around in the sand and dirt were the indolent and unemployed braves, while their filthy and vermin-covered offspring played naked in the sand. These so-called braves wore nothing but a narrow strip of cloth around their loins. While we were still camping in Denver, the warriors who had gone out to give battle to the Utes returned, bringing with them a number of horses captured from the enemy, and making both night and day hideous with their pow-wows and secret incantations. The dismal wailing and howling of the squaws, bringing back from the fight their dead and wounded, made the surroundings anything but cheerful.

Before our arrival, and imagining Denver to be a city with some pretensions to civilization, I had confided to my husband my intention of making a more prepossessing toilet before appearing on its streets. I carefully donned my best riding habit, and made myself as comely as circumstances would allow. Mounting my horse sidewise in the saddle, which I had hitherto ridden astride, I gaily rode through the one street of the town until we crossed a rude bridge, spanning Cherry creek. Here our wayward cattle balked. A loud crack from the swirling whip urging them on frightened my "Rosinante," who gave his accustomed squat, and I found myself ingloriously dismounted and lying at full length on the boards of the bridge. I was quickly lifted up by a chivalrous miner. After this ignominious debut I was only too glad to retire from sight under the cover of our wagon until we found a place to locate. We drove across the stream and camped on the banks of the Cherry creek opposite the village. We were very much discouraged by the outlook and the surroundings. The whole town seemed to be in a turmoil. In front of our camp on the other side of the creek we witnessed the hanging of two men by the Vigilance Committee. This filled me with horror and dismay, although doubtless they deserved it, for the town was overflowing with vile characters.

During our short stay in Denver we removed the bed of the wagon from off the running gear, to make some necessary repairs, and placed it upon the ground. One morning James had gone into the town to purchase some needed supplies, leaving me and my little son alone in camp, although other campers were in our vicinity. I had baked my day's supply of bread and placed it in the back of the wagon to cool. Seating myself in the front of the wagon bed, for more privacy I had drawn my curtains while I sat busily mending and conversing with my child. Suddenly, without sound or warning, my curtain was rudely pulled aside and there before me stood a huge, repulsive-looking Indian demanding bread. His tone and manner was so insolent and overbearing that it aroused my ire, and although frightened I assumed a brave front and quickly told him I had no bread to give him. He said, "You heap lie. Plenty bread," at the same time pointing to my cooling loaves, but I shook my head and gave him to understand that he could not have it. My brother's gun stood within the wagon close beside me. The Indian readied in as if to take it, but I anticipated his thoughts, and seizing the gun, placed it beyond his reach. While his gaze was fixed upon me in open-eyed wonder, I also had time to look him over and saw hanging at his belt a number of bleeding scalps taken in the last fight with the Utes. These he loosened for my closer inspection and handing them to me, told or tried to tell in his broken jargon of English and Indian what a brave chieftain he was. Keeping up the show of courage I had assumed for the occasion, but inwardly quaking, I took the bunch of bloody scalps in my hands and counted them, taking care, however, that my hands should not come in contact with the blood. The Indian looked amazed and surprised at my temerity, and with the startled exclamation, "Humph, white squaw no fear," left me as suddenly as he came.

The people that inhabited the embryo city of Denver were a most diverse and varied lot. Every class of citizen was represented. Doctors, lawyers, merchants, stage drivers, gamblers and preachers, were all in evidence and from the general style of dress it was difficult to make a distinction. All alike wore the red flannel shirt of the miner and ox driver. The most prosperous lawyer or the most successful business man or merchant was as roughly garbed as the commonest laborer. Low drinking saloons were to be seen on every hand, and gambling dens of every kind abounded. Many of the squalid adventurers lived in the crudest manner, with no law save that enacted by the Vigilance Committee. No wonder that so many coming into this dismal village, chafed and irritated with their long journey, were disheartened and discouraged and turned their faces homewards. Miners and laborers were constantly coming into Denver from the various mining districts with conflicting reports. We hardly knew whom or what to believe. Many of them were out of money and out of heart. Others who had been more fortunate told of the rich strikes they had made.

We met and talked with a number of these more optimistic prospectors who had recently come down for more supplies from a place that was then known as "Gregory's Diggings." Their encouraging reports of gold discovered re-kindled the ardor of my brother, who thus far on our journey had been satisfied to stay with us, but who now decided that he was tired of travel, and was persuaded to go back with the prospectors to the mines. Taking with him a few tools and a stock of provisions and with high hopes that he was to make his fortune in a little while and return home a rich man, he started for the mines. He was as sanguine and eager as if none had ever failed. I dreaded to part with him and leave him in that wild country to battle with all the privations that must come to adventurous prospectors in their search for gold. All men were not fitted by nature for gold diggers, and this brother of mine, — hitherto a pampered and petted darling, just from college, unused to hardships, — what dangers menaced his footsteps. What trials lay in wait for him! But no pleadings of mine were of any avail, so I bade him God speed and we parted in Denver on the banks of Cherry creek. Long afterwards I heard that after he had suffered untold privations and dangers, at last by weary stages of slow travel, sometimes on foot, he reached home, a sadder, poorer, but a wiser man.

I have mentioned our great disappointment in the village of Denver and its environment as we then found it in the summer of eighteen sixty. My husband said to me after bidding my brother farewell, "What are we going to do? Shall we remain here, return home, or push on to California?" My pride would not consent to turn my face homeward, although my heart yearned to do so, and I was so utterly disgusted with Denver and its squalid surroundings; with the Arapahoes who had made the last two or three nights indescribably hideous; with the combined drunkenness and rioting that existed everywhere in this society composed of the roughest classes of all states and nations; with this log city of maybe two hundred dwellings, not half of them completed, and the other half not fit to be inhabited by any self-respecting woman, that I felt life amid such surroundings would be to me unendurable. Without argument or hesitation, I said, "We will go on to California."

By this time we had come nearly to the bottom of our very limited purse. We had our wagon loaded with plenty of provisions, enough and more to last us for a continued journey to California. Yet we could not think of going farther without ready money to pay for the numerous ferries and other incidentals that were likely to occur on the road. So here we had to consider ways and means to replenish our scanty hoard, and to see what we could spare from our scanty belongings that could be disposed of to the best advantage. The weather was growing colder as we advanced further into the mountains. Hitherto we had traveled without a tent. We now found that we could no longer dispense with that comfort, and we must provide a camp stove for use in rainy weather. Among our stores we had packed two cases of thin, cut glass goblets and wine glasses, which were cumbersome and heavy, so we decided to lighten our load of them and strengthen our purse. James approached one of the best saloons that infested the town and told the proprietor of his wish to dispose of them to the best advantage. As freight of all kinds had to be brought overland, articles of that variety were in great demand and expensive as well. The saloon man at once offered him a very satisfactory price for all the glassware, enough to warrant us to make the necessary purchases for the comfort of our extended journey, and money sufficient to last, as we hoped, until we arrived at our destination in California.

After re-packing and re-adjusting our load, we two alone with our little son took up the lonely march through seemingly endless mountain chains, and over desert lands for more hundreds of weary miles toward the land of the setting sun. Our road led over what was then known as the "Cherokee Trail" which we had learned formed the shortest practical route from Denver to Salt Lake City.

CHAPTER VIII.

Toward Laramie—Fording A Dangerous Stream—celebrating The Fourth Of July—Entertaining Strangers—An Indian Village On The Move

We camped the first night out from Denver beside a small rippling stream, whose waters as they flowed over the pebbly bottom fell soothingly on the ear, while from its deeper pools I caught the most delicious fish I ever ate. The night was cool and breezy, but within our now comfortable tent, we set up our little camp stove and built our fire. We soon crawled in under our blankets, said our prayers to the stars that brightly twinkled through the trees overhead, and thought of home and the comfortable beds we had left so far behind us.

For several days we pushed on through a reasonably level country, though we encountered many deep, steep-banked, dry gullies, and some very rough roads, until we arrived at last at the banks of the Cache-la-Poudre river, seventy or eighty miles from Denver and by far the most formidable stream we had met. We had been told that a rope ferry was stationed here that would enable us to cross this stream with safety. Unluckily on our arrival we found that it had gone down the stream and nothing had since been heard of it. An old scout, whom we met here, assured us that there was no safe crossing for our team, as the current was very swift. If we were venturesome enough to try to ford it our wagon and cattle would be carried down stream. Here was a dilemma. We dared to go no further without assistance, though anxious to pursue our journey with some degree of haste, prudence warned us that to cross an unknown stream alone was taking too many risks. We decided to wait and see what would turn up. A merciful providence had helped us before through many an obstacle. Why not trust once more? Here we prepared to camp for an indefinite period, as there were few people, if any, coming or going over this desolate road.

At the close of the second day of our waiting there appeared, mounted on powerful horses, a white man and two Indians, trappers, coming from their isolated cabin in the heart of the Rocky mountains. They stayed with us an hour or more, sharing our evening meal. We begged their assistance in our perplexity, and they promised us if we would await their return the next day they would help us ford the uncertain stream. Of course we waited for them, for we could not help ourselves, though we feared that they might not return for our relief. However our breakfast was scarcely over the next morning when our eyes were gladdened by the sight of them returning with their horses loaded with pelts. These they hastily unloaded, and mounting their horses, they plunged into the stream, swimming them up and down until they found a reasonably safe crossing and a secure landing place, where our team with their help could reach the opposite shore with safety. Then tying a rope to the heads of our two lead oxen, a man on each side on their strong horses, we went boldly down into the deep and turbid stream. Anxiously we watched each move of the fearless horsemen as they measured the depths of the foaming stream. The current was strong and swift, and should accident happen, fatal disaster seemed almost certain. Committing our all into the hands of our Heavenly Father, we rode down into what might have been the chasm of death, where the rapid current, yawning to receive us in its cold depths, seemed ready to bury us from sight. Owing to the steepness of the bank we came near upsetting the wagon as we entered the stream, but the second Indian rode by the wagon side and dexterously righted it. The water was deep for about fifty yards or more, the bottom broken and filled with huge boulders, and the current swift and strong. I crouched in the wagon with my little son trembling with fear, while my husband, riding the ox nearest the wheel, urged his swimming cattle on. Luckily our wagon bed was not afloat, although the water came up into it. When the brave oxen pulled us up the steep banks safe once more, I uttered a prayer of thanksgiving and gladly helped unload and dry out some of our goods that had got wet in the crossing. With many and heartfelt thanks to the obliging trio, who refused any other remuneration, we bade adieu to them, as they again mounted their horses, re-crossed the stream and went on their way. Another day's delay waiting for our goods and wagon to dry out, and we resumed our interrupted journey.

The Cherokee trail, over which we were traveling, soon ran into the mountains near the Cache-la-Poudre, and henceforth for many weary miles we did not come across, neither were we overtaken by any emigrant or others moving westward. While in camp near this river I could not help but wonder at the beauty of the grand scenery surrounding us on all sides. Above us was the bright dome of a heaven so free from all earthly smoke and vapor, so clear and transparent, that the stars seemed closer and shone with an exceeding brilliancy. The air was filled with a balmy sweetness, and yet so limpid and clear that even in the starlight we could catch faint glimpses of the shimmering trees in the distant river. Our camp fire leaped up and roared in great flames, as if it, too, tasted the unlimited oxygen in the atmosphere. Beyond its bright light, purple, black and gray bluffs towered up in the clear, dark sky. The silence was profound, broken only now and then by a yelp from a coyote as he sneaked warily beyond the gleam of our fire. The river flowed at our feet, hurrying on its way over rocks and boulders and bars of sandy debris, carrying its message of melody from Rocky mountain snows to the Gulf and broad Atlantic. When at last our tired eye-lids were closed, we slept as profoundly as if we were in our own bed-chamber.

On this part of our journey we encountered many bad roads. In fact they were only trails, crossing high and rugged hills, deep ravines with rough and jagged sides, dark and dismal canyons between towering mountains. Many times we forced our way over the rocks that had fallen during the heavy rains from their steep slopes, and had to cross streams filled with boulders and choked with brush and fallen timber. Frequently we chained and double-locked our wagon wheels to prevent them crashing down some long and steep incline, and often a fallen tree lay across our path that had to be hewn and lifted by main strength. For days our progress would not average eight or ten miles. At times we came to a mountain up whose rugged slope it was almost impossible for our straining animals to pull the wagon. My husband would be at the oxen's heads urging and encouraging them in the fearful pull, while I followed closely behind the wagon carrying a big stone with which to block the wheels when the cattle stopped to blow and rest.

While traveling through the mountains between Denver and Laramie we had determined on keeping the Fourth of July as a grand holiday. I had taught my little son all the patriotic songs that I knew, brought forth from my goods and chattels our American flag and decorated our wagon and tent with the red, white and blue, regretting our lack of firecrackers or fireworks. Prom our limited larder I made preparations for a holiday dinner. We had camped the night before the Fourth in a little fertile valley, surrounded on all sides by high mountains. Many of the higher peaks were covered with snow, but down in this little valley the air was balmy and mild as a Fourth of July day should be. Here we picked our first wild strawberries, a luxury indeed to our appetites cloyed to satiety with salt bacon and beans. Our bill of fare was constructed on very simple lines yet I do not think it would have been unacceptable even to a pampered epicure. A day or two previous we had bartered with an Indian a pound of sugar for a leg of antelope. For our first course we had antelope soup, then roast antelope, and a piece of boiled ham with a curry of rice and our last can of tomatoes. I also made some very palatable cookies, even without the eggs which were considered so very necessary in their make up. Stewed dried fruit and the fresh strawberries formed our dessert, and with an excellent cup of coffee completed a meal that anyone might enjoy, notwithstanding that the cups and dishes were of tin, and our table a board over an humble and empty soap box.

We had hardly finished this bountiful repast when up the narrow defile that led into this little valley, we saw approaching us two white men on horseback, leading two horses. They informed us that they were prospectors on their way back to Denver, all they possessed being the few provisions and blankets that were packed on their extra horses. They requested our hospitality for the night, which we gladly gave them. It was often our good fortune to meet with a trapper or scout or some wandering prospector from whom we could get some useful information. I was glad I had such a good dinner for them. When they had finished eating there was not enough left to feed the birds. They very feelingly remarked that it was the best meal they had eaten since they had left their homes in the far East. We knew not whether they were friends or foes, but treated them as royally as we could. Next morning they started over their lonely road for Denver.

The next night brought a change of spirit for our camp was pitched near a little village of Indians whom we had been warned were very hostile to emigrants, and we were truly at their mercy for they were a warlike band. While I was preparing our evening meal the chief and a number of his braves came and sat down in a semi-circle around our camp fire and asked in their broken way and by signs for coffee, sugar, and "bishkit." I gave what I could from the quantity already cooked, and James gave them some tobacco to smoke. After sitting and smoking in silence one got up and went away followed at intervals by another, until finally we were left alone. How anxiously we spent that night none can ever know who have never been exposed to the dangers of savage life. Our fears proved groundless and the next morning we passed through their camp. They were making preparations to break up their own encampment. Having a large band of ponies they were compelled to move farther on for newer and more abundant pasturage.

This was our first sight of a moving Indian village and a more novel, curious, animated scene I never witnessed. I was quite indignant while I watched the indifferent braves lounging carelessly around, unmindful of the labor of their poor, overworked squaws — the former too proud and disdainful to assist the squaws in their burden of taking down their lodges, dismantling their camp, and loading their various trappings upon their primitive means of transportation, drawn by ponies and dogs. A number of lodge poles were fastened to the sides of the ponies, the ends of which trailed on the ground and on these poles, behind the animal, was fastened a light frame work interlaced with slips of rawhide, which formed a sort of platform. Over this strong trellis of rawhide and frame work were spread buffalo robes, the paraphernalia of their camp, and their most treasured clothing. On top of all were stowed their papooses and young puppies. The whole, camp with the exception of the stolid and lazy braves was in motion. Squaws, dogs, and ponies were all on the alert and moving, ready to leave the old camp for the new. The women trudged patiently along by the litter that carried their offspring. These youngsters, strapped to their straight boards with their uncovered eyes blinking in the sun, looked anything but comfortable, yet I do not remember of ever hearing an Indian baby cry or murmur. Occasionally a squaw, becoming weary with her long walk after her arduous labor of loading up the animals, would mount the litter to rest or nurse her papoose. This method of riding was said to be very comfortable as the elasticity of the supporting poles made the motion easy. A number of these litters were prepared for the aged and infirm braves and others who had been crippled in their numerous combats, and this was their only mode of locomotion. They had to be assisted on and off by their ever faithful squaws, who drove the animals as well. The numerous dogs that infested all Indian encampments were made to do duty on these occasions, and a similar equipment to that of the horses, bat on a smaller scale, was attached to them, on which were loaded the lighter articles of the camp.

We followed on in the wake of these moving aborigines until our noon halt, while they continued on their way to their further abiding place. The chief remained behind with us, waiting, no doubt, for an invitation to our mid-day meal, to which we felt compelled to invite him, very much to his satisfaction. After filling his capacious stomach to repletion and eating as much as three men would take at a meal, he arose and tried to express his gratification by rubbing his stomach with great gusto. It was characteristic of the Indians, whenever an opportunity offered, to lay in a supply of food against any future fasts. Evidently our hospitality and courteous treatment won their hearts, for they showed no signs of hostility to us. In fact from their general demeanor they rather inspired us with a confidence which seemed to sanction our presence in their midst.

CHAPTER IX.

The Rocky Mountains—Cheyenne Pass—Lost Cattle Restored—Crossing The Chugwater— Shoeing Lame Oxen—Arriving At Fort Laramie

I CANNOT now remember how many times we crossed that wonderful river, the North Platte and its tributaries. It seemed to roam hither and thither at its own sweet will. It appeared quite a torrent as it rushed out of some deep canyon, clear as crystal and cold as ice, and again it was a wide stream filled with small islands, and except at the melting of the snows in the spring, one could almost wade across it. The Indian name for this river was "Weeping Water," but tradition said that the name had been changed to Platte for a woman missionary who was very much beloved by a tribe of Pawnee Indians. During high water the crossing of this river was very dangerous, owing to the quicksands and the continual changing of the channel. Usually in the vicinity of the fords men were stationed whose business it was to see emigrants and their cattle safely over, often at a tax of eight or ten dollars a wagon. Occasionally we would arrive at the banks of the stream and find the ferryman away from his post, and much against our will were compelled to wait his return. We made the welkin ring with our shouts and halloas to bring back the missing guide.

At one of these crossings of the Platte the ferryman advised us to take the trail leading more to the north than west, in order to more quickly reach the opening of Cheyenne Pass, thereby saving us several days' hard driving over a mountainous country. We arose at the dawning of day and with an early start, hoped to reach the entrance of the Pass by nightfall, but the drive proved as usual to be longer than we expected, and the miles lengthened out until we found ourselves at night in a barren, inhospitable spot, where the feed was not abundant. James here tied two yoke of our oxen together in pairs and let them roam in order to get sufficient sustenance on the scanty feeding ground. The remaining, two oxen he had picketed with long ropes, thinking that the loose cattle would not wander far away from them. Imagine our dismay when we woke the next morning to find no sign of the other stock. This was not an agreeable, prospect, as we could not hope to recover or replace our faithful animals. What were we to do? I was afraid to be left alone while my husband went in search of them, and I greatly feared for his safety in the uncertain chase. I watched him leave me with feelings of doubt and anguish, but we both knew there was no alternative as we could go no farther with only the one remaining yoke. So mounting the horse, he ascended the range of mountains beyond us, and there to his wonder, saw an Indian driving the loose stock towards our camp. James halted until the Indian reached him, not knowing what was awaiting him, but the Indian on his near approach, by making signs and pointing backwards, implied that he had found the wandering cattle in the range beyond. James turned at once and came back to camp, the Indian following with the cattle. On reaching our camp the Indian, catching up the rope with which he had tied our cattle together, placed it in my husband's hands. We were overjoyed and surprised at the manner of their restoration and wondered greatly that the Indian, who had us completely in his power, had returned them in that way.

It truly seemed to us in our long journey traveling alone that the Indians watched over us. Perhaps our utter loneliness and unprotected position, showing them that we had the most implicit confidence in them awoke in their breasts a feeling of chivalrous protection. Our confidence and resolution in the face of overpowering numbers may have won their regard. Be that as it may, in our ignorant fearlessness we came through the many hostile tribes unmolested and unhurt, while we heard details of various raids against emigrants who had preceded us. I was led to believe that the tribes with whom we came in contact had some secret sign whereby they communicated with one another, for we frequently noticed the smoke of fires on different heights as we traveled or stopped at our numerous camps. Sometimes the smoke would ascend straight up into the air in columns, at other times it would be diffused and wavering. By degrees learning then and long after that this was their method of communicating with each other at a distance, we at last came to the conclusion that in this or some other way the Indians had taken charge of us. With feeling of gratitude at the kindly action of the Indian, who had brought our wandering stock back to us, I prepared a bountiful breakfast, for I had learned that the way to a red man's heart lay in the same direction as that of his more civilized brother, and I have never found an appeal to the stomach in vain. I even made extra efforts to whet his ever-ready appetite. I made my lightest flap-jacks, browned them with the lovely hue that made them most inviting, sprinkled them with sugar so tempting to the Indians, and poured cup after cup of my aromatic coffee, which evidently from the number he drank, fully satisfied his critical tastes, while slice after slice of bacon and beans without stint went into his capacious stomach. I wondered if he had eaten anything for a month, so marvelous was the quantity that disappeared. He stayed with us until we left camp and started out on our day's travel. I gave him a loaf of the warm bread I had baked and a piece of bacon to take with him. He followed us for a while, then took his departure down the canyon and was lost to view.

As we proceeded northward toward the main line of overland travel, our route lay over a badly gullied region, and we crossed many streams emerging from the mountains. By one of these our trail ran for more than forty miles, and in its tortuous windings we crossed it many times. The Red Buttes were conspicuous all along this river. The earth which gave them their peculiar color was said to be rich in iron. On the lower bottoms of this stream the grass was luxuriant, but the mosquitoes and gnats swarmed in such numbers that our stock could neither feed nor rest, while the annoyance to ourselves was more than tantalizing. Finding it impossible to sleep in this camp, we arose early and drove eight or ten miles before we could leave the persecuting horde of insects behind us. We drove until we came to a most excellent spring of clear, cold water, unimpregnated with any trace of alkali, and the best water we had drunk since leaving Clear creek west of Denver. Most of the many streams we had crossed were muddy and tasted more or less of the ever present alkali.

Finding it necessary to repair our wagon we stayed at this spring for two or three days. It was a most picturesque spot, lying between rows of magnificent buttes looking in the distance, like ruined castles, some of them perpendicular and circular in form. They presented a variegated and fantastic appearance when viewed from a distance. In spots they were brilliant vermillion, but when broken by the water courses passing over them, they presented uneven surfaces of white clay, which gave them their peculiar appearance. After leaving these larger buttes, our road gradually descended until we reached the banks of a ravine, where we had great difficulty in getting down to the bed of the stream. Unyoking the forward oxen, leaving only the wheel oxen attached to the wagon, we chained and locked our wagon wheels, but even with all these precautions we came to grief, for the heavy wagon rushing down the steep incline, caused the oxen to swerve in such a manner that the wheels cramped and the wagon was thrown against a mound of earth and loose rock that partly held it from a complete upset. Here we were in a deep ravine with no help near. We could neither get out nor go on. Not a spot of ground was level enough to stand upon in any comfort. The wagon had to be unloaded before it could be righted, and as the noon hour had passed there was a prospect of spending the night in this gloomy cavern. There was no other alternative but for both of us to go to work and unload as soon as possible. Even unloaded the wagon was too much for one man to lift. James rigged up a sort of lever and with the help of the oxen, managed to right it again and pull the half empty wagon to a place less steep and more secure farther down the slope. By the time we had carried our goods down the hill to the wagon and reloaded it, it was near sundown. Hitching on all the oxen, we drove down into the narrow and deep stream. The opposite side was fully as steep and it required the combined strength of our cattle to pull us up the bank. This stream was called the Chugwater, where we spent the night, expecting in a few days to arrive at Laramie.

Before reaching Laramie we drove one night into a little park at the base of a mountain. It was almost a semi-circle, rimmed with dark and forbidding mountains. A small stream winds its way along its timbered banks. There seemed to be a strange witchery in this place. The wind moaned and wailed most sadly. All through the night we imagined we heard strange sighs above and around us. We could hear stealthy trampings which seemed to come from other beasts than those that drew us on our journey. While we were stopping in Laramie, a soldier told us that this peculiar spot was called the

"Haunted Hole of the Black Elk." Perhaps if we had known that this little park had such an uncanny reputation, we might have pushed farther on for our night's rest. However nothing harmed us, and only the huge mountains that surrounded us so closely overpowered us with their immensity.

The next morning, long before the sun's rays could penetrate this little dell, we were prepared to push onward, but not with great speed, for we were to climb another mountain up whose steep ascent we were to lift ourselves over two thousand feet. In one place we wound around tall, ragged cliffs. The soil was loose and unstable, composed of pulverized debris and shaly rock, which kept constantly slipping, so that the oxen had great difficulty in keeping their footing. It had been a steep and tiresome climb. For a time we had been riding in the wagon but the way seemed so rough and dangerous, that to assure our safety, we alighted, and very fortunately, for in less than twenty yards further, the rear wheels of the wagon began to slip over the shelving embankment, and it was with almost miraculous effort that our brave cattle pulled the wagon beyond the danger point. Every moment I expected to see it topple over the precipice, pulling our valiant oxen with it. James plied his ox goad more furiously than our cattle had ever felt before, but it was the time for greater effort, and after the danger was past he almost wept over the cruel blows he gave our gallant team. Weary from the excitement of this clay, probably more than the fatigue, we went into camp, I made great effort to be cheerful and happy and tried to laugh away the remembrance of the peril through which we had passed, but all through the night in my fitful slumbers I had visions of the towering cliff, and in my broken dreams felt the motion of the treacherous soil giving way over the sloping walls of the precipice.

While traversing this slope of the Rocky mountains we climbed numberless ridges and penetrated many passes, descending one lofty plateau only to encounter another. One morning we struck an almost level plain which appeared several miles in extent. There was only a dim trail to follow, growing fainter as we proceeded, until we finally lost it altogether. The grass on this plain, though coarse, grew thick and close. The way had been little traveled that season and the heavy growth had obliterated all signs of the trail. We wandered over this plateau for hours, trying to keep our northerly course, growing more fearful every moment that we were lost. At last we discovered afar off a fringe of trees, denoting a stream. On reaching it we drove up and down its timbered banks, when to our great relief we again struck our lost trail at the ford. We named this stream, "Lost Trail creek," but it should have been "Box Elder," so thickly were its borders covered with a growth of those trees.

Crossing this stream we again ascended a high, rocky, barren plain, and for two or three days the trail led us over a most peculiar formation, composed of large pebbles, averaging the size of a goose egg. Our cattle became foot-sore traveling this rough roadway. Their hoofs were worn almost to the quick. They could no longer travel with any degree of haste, and it was truly pitiful to watch their limping efforts. We decided, to stop at the first water we came to and give them a chance to rest. It was almost dark that night before we came to a little spring near the roadside, and as soon as the poor brutes were unyoked, they immediately lay down in their tracks, and for several hours neither ate nor drank, so weary and footsore were they.

Next morning on looking down from our lofty camp into the small valley below us, we discovered a tiny cabin and a wreath of smoke issuing from its wide chimney. This cabin, though rough and primitive, denoted the presence of the white man. Our curiosity soon grew beyond bounds and the next day we yoked up our lame team and drove down to investigate. We found two grizzled, old mountaineers located in this fertile valley. They had a small herd of cattle with which they supplied the nearest forts with beef. They informed us that they had lived in this lonely place for four or five years, seeing no one for months at a time, except the few emigrants who passed during the summer season, or when driving their stock to the forts. They had built a rude forge, where they shod their own horses and those of passing emigrants. From them we learned that we could have our lame cattle shod with heavy leather shoes. This detained us however for two or three days as each ox had to be tied and thrown during the shoeing process. But it enabled them to travel in comfort for many miles before it had to be repeated.

Perhaps I have tediously described this cross march from Denver, before we reached the high road that led to California. This part of our journey was the only portion not traversed by mail, stage or pony express. It lay through a region in which there were few white settlers but the providence which had been with us from the beginning, safely guided us through all the perils that might have beset our path. After many days we arrived at Fort Laramie from where we were to follow the regular overland road to California. We forded the swollen Laramie river in the early twilight and camped on its farther shore, feeling thankful that the loneliness which had hitherto oppressed us over the Cherokee trail and through Cheyenne Pass was removed. Though young and inexperienced, I had learned to adapt myself to the rough life of an emigrant, — crossing swollen streams, encountering terrific storms and dreading constantly an attack from hostile Indians. But an American women well born and bred is endowed with the courage of her brave pioneer ancestors, and no matter what the environment she can adapt herself to all situations, even to the perilous trip across the western half of this great continent, ever ready to wander over paths which women reared in other countries would fear to follow.

CHAPTER X.

While we were camping near Fort Laramie, the soldiers warned us of danger. A detachment had been sent out from the fort on a reconnoitering expedition and reported an attack of Indians on an emigrant company of eight men, whom they had killed or taken prisoners, burnt their wagons and taken their mules and horses. These soldiers also informed us of the approach of a train of emigrants of about sixty men with a large number of horses and wagons. The officer at the fort insisted on our remaining in its vicinity until the arrival of that company, as we were running recklessly into danger traveling alone. Deciding that it would perhaps be wiser to heed his counsel, we waited and in due time the large caravan made its appearance and we joined their company.

This proved to be the most unhappy part of our journey. Hitherto we had proceeded at our own sweet will. Accustomed to traveling alone, we stopped when and where we pleased, and started out in the same manner. Now all was changed. It was the custom for every large company of emigrants to select from their number a captain. His word was law. Every one belonging to that company was supposed to do and act as he ordered. We were obliged to keep our place in the moving caravan, travel as long and as fast as he thought best, and camp when and where he chose. Previous to this time we had made shorter drives and stopped before dark. With this company, we frequently drove until after nightfall. This was to me an unaccustomed hardship. Cooking in camp by daylight, was no easy task, and darkness made it still more difficult. Our campfires were often of sage brush which emitted only evanescent flames. Our lanterns dimly lighted with one small candle made only a glimmer in the darkness of the wilderness. My husband, too, had always been with me at night, but now had to take his turn as night watchman, and my little son and I would be left in our tent alone, while he was posted as sentinel on the outskirts of our encampment. Never before had I suffered with fear as I did while with that company. I could not rest or sleep while my husband was away from me, exposed to all the perils of the night and the treacherous foe. We might have been in the same danger before, but we were together.

My fears were not only of Indians. These people with whom we were traveling were the roughest, most uncouth and ignorant people that I had ever come in contact with. Perfectly lawless, fighting and quarreling among themselves, using language terrible to hear, they were the champion swearers of the world. They swore at their wives, at their horses, at each other, at the wind that blew, at the stones in the road. The air was constantly filled with their curses. The women of the company were fitting mates for the men. The whole company was made up of outlaws from Texas, Arkansas and Southwestern Missouri. They imagined that they were so strong in numbers that they could whip any band of Indians, and it was their usual custom whenever the Indians approached our camp or sat by our camp fires to tease and play various tricks upon them. I noticed on different occasions that the Indians looked on their manoeuvers with a resentful glare, and conversed with each other in low muttered tones, and I trembled with fear for what they might do in retaliation. Many times I tried to expostulate with these mien, but they laughed with scorn, saying they were not afraid of any band of Indians.

Very soon their bravado was put to the test. At the close of one day's long travel we had barely set our camp for the night, when a lone, frightened pony express rider came galloping in haste into our camp, shouting to us that the Indians were near and would very soon attack us. While he was descending into a little canyon they had suddenly come upon him from their ambush, pursued and shot at him several times, and only that his horse was fresh and faster had he been able to escape them. Every minute we were expecting to hear the blood-curdling yells of the approaching foe. For the first few moments after the report reached us, the men who had hitherto boasted of their fearlessness were palsied with fright; however they soon rallied and made hasty preparations to meet and repel the attack. It was a night long to be remembered. Here indeed was a grave and perilous situation — overloaded wagons, tired horses and oxen, defenseless women and children. For what power was there in the hands of a few white men against a horde of Indians, bent on murder and robbery, and coming so suddenly on our far-away camp in the wilderness, most of whose numbers were defenseless women and children?

Our wagons had been arranged in the usual semi-circle enclosing the camp. Our animals were brought within and picketed as closely as possible. The men hurriedly put their guns in order. The women held their children closely to their breasts not knowing how soon they would be ruthlessly torn from them and dashed to death or put to torture before their eyes. After hours of suspense we began to hope that our fears were groundless, but this hope was soon dashed from our minds by the startling cry from another messenger, that an attack from the opposite side was momentarily expected. Every ear was listening for the sound of the fleet feet of their ponies, every heart throbbing with anxious fear, but every lip was silent. At this hour a fearful storm of rain and hail with continued thunder and lightning fell upon us. The sharp hail and the continued peals of thunder so frightened our restless stock that there was imminent danger of a stampede. The pelting rain flowed into our frail tents, wetting our pillows and blankets. At any other time this would have been considered a great misfortune. Now we hardly noticed it, while we sat through that terrible night, drenched to the skin, beaten upon by the gusts of wind and hail, deafened by the continuous peals of thunder, every moment expecting the attack of the lurking foe. The darkness was so complete that we might have been surrounded by hundreds of the demons and yet been none the wiser, and the uproar of the storm was so loud that hearing was as useless as sight. No one slept save the little children. The night which seemed interminably long at last passed away and morning showed no enemy in sight. My husband and I uttered a fervent prayer of thanksgiving. No doubt the fearful storm had caused the attack to be abandoned.

In the course of a few hours we ventured on our way, hoping that we were not to be molested. Our number of nearly sixty men marched with loaded rifles each side of the wagons to guard the women and children who were huddled closely within. The day was long and anxious and nightfall brought us little relief, for our next halt was among the charred remains of an express station which had been burnt by the savage foe. Half our men stood guard, while the others slept with their ready guns at hand.

The now frightened emigrants with whom we were traveling were more civil and subdued in their manner. This lasted for a few days, but as the fear of an immediate attack from the Indians wore away they resumed their usual tactics. They quarreled among themselves and were brutal and domineering to their wives, never caring for their comfort or well-being. The captain of the company was a tyrannical, ignorant man, who ruled with an iron hand. His every effort was to impress all that he was paramount and every one must obey. It was he that regulated the length of the day's travel, selected the camp, formed the corral at night, appointed the guards and arbitrated all disputes. My hot Southern blood soon rebelled at his imperious and despotic rule. Every day about an hour before camping time he rode with two or three of his henchmen a mile or two ahead of the wagon train and selected our camping place for the night. His selections were frequently very unwise and uncomfortable. Sometimes his choice was a side hill, and our beds would slope too much for comfort, or a rocky spot by the road when a few rods either side would be smoother or less rugged. But whatever the discomforts, where he decided there we camped. One night I felt it necessary to assert myself and renounce his petty authority. We had driven many miles that day over a long rough road and all were tired and hungry. When we came to the place where we were to pitch our tents, we found that it had been occupied the night before by emigrants who had preceded us from all appearances with a great number of stock. Within twenty rods of the place selected was a clear, grassy spot and just as near the water. A number of the women, although grumbling at the filth, prepared to make their lowly beds, while the men hurriedly raised the tents. My husband drove his team into the wagon stockade as usual. I said to him in an undertone, "You need not unhitch your oxen in this place. I will not camp here." He replied "If we do not obey the rules of the company we will have to leave it." "All right," I said, "The sooner the better it will suit me. I would rather trust myself to the mercy of the Indians than to travel another day with these ruffians and their ignorant captain. If you do not drive me to a cleaner place to camp and sleep tonight I will take my blankets and go alone." He knew full well that I meant to do as I said. So without another word he turned his team and drove to the place I selected. The other women looked on my daring insubordination with wondering eyes, and, envious of my cleanly quarters, at last plucked up courage to follow my example, and with much profanity the camp was moved. That night James and I held council together and we decided to withdraw from the company, feeling that we were safer and more comfortable traveling alone.

The next morning when the order was given to break camp and all were busy preparing to move onward except ourselves, we remained quiet in camp. Some of the more friendly women offered me their assistance, thinking I was not well. I thanked them kindly and assured them I was well, but felt tired and needed a longer rest, and that it was our intention to remain in camp until we were thoroughly rested. The men jeered at us and said by nightfall our scalps would hang at the belt of some wild Indian. We paid but little heed to their remarks. Finally perceiving that we were indeed going to stay behind, the captain gave the command and the big caravan drove on leaving us alone in the wilderness. We remained in camp two days, giving them an opportunity to get so far ahead that we might never overtake them or see them again. Alone in the wilderness, we felt more secure and far happier than when travelling with this uncongenial band. Afterwards we heard repeated rumors that they had been attacked and almost annihilated.

From Laramie for some distance we encountered no one save Indians. It was a barren and desolate region. Off to our left were the Black Hills, so called because they were covered with a dense growth of pine, cedar and hemlock trees which gave them a dark and forbidding appearance. Farther to the south, at a distance of thirty miles or more arose Laramie Peak, towering up to a height said to be over six thousand feet. The milky streams in the neighborhood of Laramie, running through the peculiar white clay soil, formed numerous buttes and bluffs, and by some strange alchemy of nature the most singular formations would crop out here and there, like ruined towers, castles and battlements. Over the facades of the numerous cliffs, strange forms and faces would stand out in bold relief.

In a few days after leaving Laramie we came to the Sweetwater river, near which we traveled for a week or ten days and owing to its tortuous course we crossed it many times before leaving it near the South Pass. I must not forget to mention a famous land mark in the valley of this river and near our road, Independence rock, so named by a party of emigrants who made their camp there on a Fourth of July in the earlier emigration of 1849 and had held a grand patriotic celebration. Many of their names had been painted on the face of the huge rock, but time and long exposure to the elements had nearly obliterated them.

This rock stood out on almost a level plain and was entirely detached from the mountains near it. In this fertile valley of the Sweetwater the grass was luxuriant, and our cattle regained the flesh and loss of strength that befell them on the rocky trails that lamed them so terribly. But soon again we struck another sixteen-mile desert and a mountain beyond, and after toiling up its long ascent and down into the little park on its further slope, we came upon a camp of weary Mormon emigrants.

These recruits of the Mormons were mostly Swedes and Norwegians and were accompanied by several Mormons who had been sent to Norway and Sweden for them and who had induced them by alluring promises to take this long and perilous trip. There were young women with them with hand carts which they had trundled all the long distance from the Missouri river. They were a most unprepossessing lot, sun burned and weather beaten and stolid. They were dressed in their old country costume of stout woolen material. They wore heavy striped yarn stockings that barely reached to the knee. Kerchiefs that had once been bright were carelessly knotted under their chins and formed their only head covering but were no protection for their faces, which were nearly as brown as the Indians', in spite of their original fair complexions. The Mormon missionary never attempted to proselyte among the rich or educated, or even among those in moderate circumstances, but always among the poorest and most ignorant, who had been born in utter misery and who had nothing to lose. These missionaries drew the most glowing pictures to the ignorant of what their lives would be in the City of the Saints — of the independence and ease that awaited them, of the freedom from privations, and of the marvelous profits to be derived from their labors. No wonder the heads of these poor creatures were turned by such proselyting, and that converts to Mormonism were continually arriving.

For several days we traveled along in sight of them and camped near them at night It gave me the heartache to see those poor girls take up their burdens every day, load up their hand carts and push them over those rugged mountains, stopping at intervals to rest their weary backs and wipe the perspiration from their dripping brows. Our conversation with them was necessarily very limited as they spoke but little English, and the Mormon men who accompanied the outfit rather discouraged any intimacy with gentiles. After a few days we passed them on the road and saw them no more.

One night somewhere between Laramie and Green river we halted at the foot of a mountain over which we had traveled laboriously all day. Early in the afternoon we discovered a spring of water and fairly good grass for our cattle. While it was too soon to make a camp on that long summer day, yet our stock seemed weary and footsore, and we ourselves were willing to take the good thus provided and go no farther. While we were pitching our tent and making preparations for camp, a team of mules and several men came in sight. They proved to be French Canadians, who like ourselves were bound for California. On reaching our camp they told us that the tribe of Indians roaming over that region was hostile, and that we were incurring great danger by remaining there alone. They insisted that we join them and go on over the next mountain. But we were tired and so were our cattle. Their proposal meant a long heavy pull probably until midnight. We had encountered no troubles with the Indians so far, why should we fear now? We advised them to tarry with us. But no, they were in a mad, wild rush to push on and bidding us farewell, went on their way.

Next morning after a refreshing and good night's rest, we were up bright and early on the road. It took us several hours before we reached the summit of the next mountain, with its remote view of the canyon below. After a while we discovered what in the distance looked like the wagon of the Canadians, but as we came nearer we could discover no sign of life or movement in their camp. No mules were browsing in sight and not a man visible. When we came within hailing distance no one greeted us. We found the wagon rifled of everything. The ground bore traces of a struggle. The mules had evidently been stampeded and the men taken prisoners to the camp of the Indians to be tortured to death. We traced the tracks of the mules and ponies for some distance in an opposite direction to the one we were traveling; but as we had met no Indians we concluded that discretion was the better part of valor, and did not extend our search, feeling only too thankful that a merciful providence had been with us. Had we taken the advice of the men I am afraid we should never have lived to tell the tale.

After leaving the Sweetwater river our road gradually led us to the beginning of the South Pass, which I imagined to be a narrow, difficult, winding gorge between towering mountains. In this I was happily mistaken, and for a few days we traveled over a road as smooth and as hard as a well kept country thoroughfare. On reaching the summit of the South Pass one could hardly believe that we were crossing the backbone of the Rocky mountains. The gradual ascent was not laborious. And here we found the dividing line between the Atlantic and the Pacific, for as we traversed several miles of rolling land two low mounds, called Twin Buttes, marked the point where all the little streams and rivers flowed toward the Pacific. I could see but little difference in the taste of the waters, the alkali flavor still predominated. In the course of a few days in our gradual descent we struck a springy marsh of fifteen or twenty acres where the ground seemed to shake as we went over it, and in the center of this morass we found the so-called Pacific springs. The water was cold and clear, but so obnoxious to the taste that I could not drink it.

Not far from the Pacific springs we struck the Oregon trail where the road branched off further to the north, while our route led us in a more southerly direction. We were now out of the South Pass, and camped one night on the treeless banks of the little Sandy river. A band of Snake Indians were in our vicinity, and according to my usual custom I prepared for company. Strange to relate not one of them approached us. This alarmed us somewhat because we had been accustomed to have them drop in upon us on all occasions, and in this seeming indifference we feared a sinister motive.

The fear of hostile Indians was not our only worry, for once again our little hoard of money was running low. The numerous ferries over the Platte and its tributaries made heavy inroads into our slender purse. On one or two occasions it had been replenished by sales of flour and bacon to emigrants who had not laid in so large a store as we, but even with that help we were at our last extremity for money. Food we had in abundance, but only coin would pay our way over a formidable stream that must be crossed by ferry and was impossible to ford. My husband, worried beyond measure at our predicament, had fretted himself almost sick. I, probably owing to my nature of blissful ignorance, took a more optimistic view of the situation and urged him not to worry. We had been told that it would cost twenty dollars to cross the Green river by ferry. I fondly hoped that the amount had been exaggerated or that some way would be provided. My trust was not in vain, for a few days before reaching that stream we were overtaken by a solitary horseman who rode by our wagon side until our noon halt. He asked my husband if he could share our noon meal with us, and said he would gladly pay for it.

He was a Frenchman by the name of Philip. We never knew any other name for him. After dinner he took my husband aside and explained why he was alone in the heart of the continent. He had fallen out with the company with which he was traveling, and taking his guns and blankets, left them, depending for food solely on the wild game he could shoot. He begged my husband to board him for a week or two until he reached his destination beyond the Green river. James felt some qualms about taking in a stranger and came to me for advice. At once I replied "Tell him we will take him for twenty dollars."

I have often thought since if we had asked a hundred he would have just as gladly have paid it, as he seemed well provided with money. He proved to be a very kindly gentleman while with us for the few days before reaching his destination, and his twenty dollars carried us well along on our journey and tided us over a precarious time. For years afterwards when the hour looked darkest and both of us were discouraged I would say "Don't worry, maybe Philip will turn up." The name was a synonym of good luck for us.

CHAPTER XI.

In due time we arrived at Green river, which we had been told was a dangerous and difficult river to ford, and that to transport our stock and wagon over its depths would take all our little hoard of money. Instead we hailed it as an oasis in the desert, for it furnished us with clear sweet water to drink, and our thirsty stock reveled in it to their hearts' content. The Green river no longer held any terrors for us. The huge flat-bottomed boat, drawn by ropes suspended from either side across the deep stream and at a price much less than we expected, safely landed us on the farther side of the stream that had been such a great bugbear to us. Here we rested a few days. The river flowed through a narrow valley. The grass, though coarse, proved to be good feed for our cattle, and the rest put new courage and endurance in their weary frames. Here, too, were green trees on which to set our tired eyes. They were only willows and cottonwoods yet we enjoyed a camp under their grateful shade.

A trading post had been established at this ferry for the few mountaineers who owned large herds of cattle. Other emigrants besides ourselves were camping here. Their broken down teams forced them to trade their worn out oxen for fresher ones on almost any terms. The mountain stockmen did a lively business with unfortunate emigrants, taking a woeful advantage of their necessity. My sympathy was strongly aroused by their distress. Two or three families had been delayed there for two weeks waiting for their cattle to get strong enough to resume their journey. Their own provisions were getting short and the season growing late, they gravely feared that they would not get through their long journey before the snow fell again on the mountains.

We became acquainted at this place with an old trader who in his earlier life had been a man of considerable polish and intelligence, but owing to

66

some unfortunate circumstances in his youth had drifted thus far over the continent in the early forties. Homeless, penniless and an outcast, he managed in some way to establish himself here at the Green river, and by slow degrees had acquired several hundred head of cattle and a considerable band of horses. With true Mormon spirit he also annexed several squaws for wives, and had any number of half breed children, who swarmed around the filthy quarters that he called home. The rude huts they occupied were in the most squalid surroundings. For many years this had been his home, yet not the slightest effort had been made to improve his mode of living. With all that fertile land surrounding him there was neither garden nor orchard. Fresh fruit and vegetables were unknown to him and his half breed family. He was said to be worth seventy-five or one hundred thousand dollars, and yet appeared to be perfectly satisfied with these most wretched conditions. Somewhere I had read that it would take only a few years for the white man to return to the aboriginal condition, and it certainly proved true in this man's case.

Most of the men who inhabited these trading posts had squaws for wives. It was quite the ordinary thing for the Indians to bring their most attractive and winsome daughters and offer them for sale to the white men. Those not quite so comely would bring thirty or forty dollars, while others more pleasing would bring sixty or seventy according to their charms. To my point of view they were the most repulsive looking creatures. I could see neither beauty, grace nor intelligence in their stolid-looking countenances. Their manners and habits were disgusting and offensive. The women thus bought and sold were no truer to their masters than their more civilized sisters of the same caste in other countries and were ever ready to decamp with any soldier or other man who offered sufficient inducements in the way of beads, blankets, or other gaudy paraphernalia. After leaving Green river at many points we would come across the discarded belongings of the emigrants who preceded us. We were enabled to form an idea of the condition of their stock, whether horses or cattle, by the goods and chattels they were continually discarding in their endeavor to lighten the burden of their overworked and worn out teams. Once by the roadside, we came across a heavy old-fashioned cook stove which some emigrant had hauled all those weary miles of mountain and desert, only to discard it at last. No doubt some poor forlorn woman was now compelled to do her cooking by the primitive camp fire, perhaps much against her will. I could imagine the heated arguments when day after day that heavy stove had to be loaded and unloaded. No doubt the air was blue many times with the volley of emphatic and profane words, hurled against that inoffensive but cumbersome article. A little wooden cradle nearby looked pathetic in its loneliness; and the tiny new made grave that we had passed a few days previous told too truly the cause of its desertion. It was no unusual sight to see wagon boxes, log chains, tires and other heavy articles abandoned to lighten the loads, and the most astonishing thing to me was that these things would lie there without attracting the notice of either Indians or herdsmen. They proved to have no value to these denizens of the wilderness.

The hills west of Green river were thinly covered with straggling groves of pines and cedars. Grass was more abundant in the little valleys, and the streams of water had lost the milky look which they acquired from the clay wash lying near the desert lands. We were still in the midst of sage brush, even in these fertile valleys, but it was no longer universal and alone. The wild currant and other shrubs became more abundant. Occasionally we came upon a little patch of land cultivated by some progressive Mormon. It was a matter of astonishment to us that the herdsmen of these fertile districts, with their cattle roaming over a thousand hills, had never experimented with cultivating the soil. They never knew the taste of cabbage or tomato. A potato was considered the greatest luxury, and was brought to the trading posts from miles away. As for cultivated fruit of any description they knew it not. We found in the canyons a wild and sour gooseberry which proved to be fairly palatable, and at intervals near the streams grew a wild grass whose succulent roots gave out the flavor of the cucumber. We had watched the Indians eating this grass, and testing it ourselves, thought it very good, but it was found rarely. I had grown very tired of bacon day after day. The very smell of beans cooking nauseates me to this day. I have never overcome my antipathy to rice in any form, while stewed prunes are still an abomination in my sight. Our diet was confined mainly to these articles. It was impossible to buy fresh vegetables on our route, and our canned fruit and vegetables had long given out. We had grown so weary of the sameness of our daily diet that the intense longing for something different grew upon us, and we looked forward anxiously to Fort Bridger where we hoped in a few days to find fresh meat and vegetables.

From Laramie westward we were in the line of the celebrated pony express, which was established in April, 1860, to carry important mail more rapidly than was possible in the overland stage. Our daily excitement was in watching for its fearless riders as they flew by us on their swift ponies. It was nearly ten years in advance of the first overland telegraph, which could not be maintained until there was a line of railroad parallel to it. The pony express was an attempt to carry letters by private service from St. Joseph, Missouri, to Sacramento, California in ten days. It was a daring enterprise to attempt to cover nearly two thousand miles of prairie, desert and mountain by solitary riders from station to station. These stations were at intervals of about thirty miles. In a year's time it proved more than human endurance could stand. The stations consisted of a rude hut for the keeper, enclosed in a high stockade where the relief ponies were corralled. The certainty of always finding water at these stations induced us to make extra efforts to camp near them at night fall. Once it became our sad duty to bury the partially burned and mutilated body of the man in charge of the station to prevent the wolves and coyotes from devouring his remains. The Indians had been there before us, killed and scalped the keeper, run off with the ponies, and left the stockade in flames. Alarming as this was, we were obliged to camp near the smoldering ruins.

One morning while we lingered near one of these stations, a rider who looked like a mere boy came flying into the post, the man whose place he filled having been killed by the Indians. The pony had made his way to the next station alone. This youth had ridden hard through the darkness of the night trying to cover both his own ground and that of the man who had been shot. He quickly changed horses, took his package of letters, and was off again on his perilous way. These brief stops at the stations were all that broke the monotony of untold hardships and danger. While the riders were young, sturdy and robust men, one of the essential requirements was that they must be of light weight, as the ponies were not expected to carry more than one hundred and fifty pounds. The superior endurance of those ponies saved many a fearless man in his race for life with roaming bands of Indians.

For some time after we had separated ourselves from our unpleasant traveling companions we traveled without adventure of any kind, and saw nothing of the Indians that were supposed to be on the war-path. We flattered ourselves that we were too near Fort Bridger to have any fears. One evening, however, as we drove into a little fertile valley, we came in sight of an encampment of the supposed foe, with a large band of ponies feeding on the rich grass. Their rude tepees were clustered near the stream within a mile of the road. Uncertain of the reception awaiting us, we made camp as usual. In a little while first one Indian then another came around our fire, until I had an audience of several watching me prepare our evening meal. I was careful to bake an extra quantity of biscuit that night, for we were so completely at their mercy I thought it wise to conciliate them in every way possible. I found it no easy task, as it required several skillets full before I had enough. James generously handed out his precious tobacco for them to smoke with him around our camp fire.

Next morning we drove away from our camp, leaving a number of them who still hung around for the last cup of coffee. As we waved our farewells to them, we noticed one of them mount his pony and follow us, not closely, but keeping us well in sight. When we stopped for our noon-day rest he soon joined us, and of course we invited him to partake of our frugal luncheon, hoping that he would return to band. But he continued to follow us until nightfall. When we prepared to camp he did likewise. Staking out his pony with the long rope of braided leather which he carried, and approaching my box of cooking utensils, he took from it the large knife I used in cooking, and pointing to some coarse grass that grew near the water he proceeded to cut and gather an armful, which he placed under our wagon and prepared his bed for the night. While alarmed and anxious we were powerless and made the best of our novel situation. I prepared a more bountiful meal when I found we were to entertain this most unwelcome guest. After eating a hearty meal, which he seemed to enjoy, he smoked a while with my husband. All this time there was no word of conversation, as neither he nor we could communicate except by signs. Finally he rolled himself beneath the wagon, and we went to rest in our little tent, but slept fitfully with one eye open the balance of the night. This continued for three days and we concluded that he had adopted us and intended to remain with us for the balance of our pilgrimage. On the evening of the third day, after replenishing his inner man with a hearty supper, he arose, caught his pony which was feeding a short distance from the camp, and, pointing backward, tried to make us understand that he was going to return to his tribe. As soon as we divined that he was about to leave us, I tied up a loaf of bread, some bacon, a cup full of sugar, and gave it to him, and we saw him depart, wondering why he came and why he went.

Not for several days was the mystery explained. Meeting an old scout at a watering place where we stopped one night, we related the circumstance to him. He told us that the country through which we were going at that time was filled with Indians who were unfriendly to emigrants, and this Indian was sent with us to show that we were under their special care and not to be molested. If that were true, it went to prove that there was honor among these savage tribes of the wilderness. Our lonely and unprotected situation must have appealed to them, and our uniform kindness was rewarded in many ways perhaps when we knew it not. At any rate we could truthfully say we never received any ill at their hands, and came through the various tribes without the loss of anything save one bright new tin tea kettle that I had bought in Denver. Its brightness proved too much of a temptation to an elderly squaw who came to visit us, and carefully seated herself beside it. It disappeared when she did under the folds of her soiled and tattered blanket.

Another circumstance I think worth mentioning here. Once in passing a group of Indians I noticed that one sat wrapped in his blanket the image of despair. The expression on his countenance showed that he was suffering great pain. My husband spoke to his squaw who was standing near and said to her, "Brave, heap sick." She shook her head but at the same time opened her mouth and pointed to her teeth, and then to the suffering brave. James approached the Indian and by signs coaxed him to open his mouth. He found the molar had a large cavity which was the cause of his suffering. I had brought with me several vials of toothache drops, for my little son had frequent attacks of toothache. Bringing forth one of the bottles containing the soothing drops and a piece of cotton, with the aid of a sharp splinter I inserted some of the remedy into the aching tooth. The effect was magical, and I was surprised to watch the change that came over the sufferer's expressive countenance. He raised his eyes that had been sternly fixed on the ground, rubbed his face slowly, then turned towards his squaw who was standing behind him watching the effect of the remedy the white squaw was employing, and in a. low tone communicated to her that the pain was relieved. Then turning to the other Indians who were grouped around, he spoke in a louder voice. In a moment we were surrounded by them eager to see the little vial that contained the magical drops. It was critically examined and passed from one to another, and although we could not understand a word, yet their expressions of gratitude were perfectly intelligible. I left the bottle and the piece of raw cotton with the Indian sufferer, for I well knew that the toothache would again return.

Another time while waiting in camp over Sunday, I had been repairing some of my husband's red flannel shirts. One was too far worn to be of any service further, and I had relegated it to the rag-bag. A number of Indian children stood around watching me at my work, and my sewing utensils seemed very curious to them. The idea came to me to fashion for them a rag doll and see what the effect would be on these stolid children of the wilderness. With a portion of white cloth taken from my work-bag, and the remains of the discarded red shirt, I made a rag baby, marking the features of the doll with colored thread. My efforts were closely watched by the curious children, and when I finished the doll I handed it to the smallest girl. At first the child did not seem to realize that she was to keep it. After each one of the children had examined it thoroughly they gave it back to me. Finally I made the little one understand that she was to keep it, and when one of the larger children attempted to take it from her, she uttered a weird cry and started off on a swift run with the rag baby hugged closely to her breast. In a little while two or three squaws came into our camp with the child and doll, and by signs asked for another. I soon discovered I would be very busy if I attempted to supply them with rag babies. But I made another for them, showing them how to do it, gave them the remains of the red flannel shirt and other pieces of cloth that I could spare, and sent them off rejoicing. This was my last effort, however, in trying either to instruct or amuse the Indians. Only on Sundays did we linger in camp long enough to have any extra time on our hands, and our inability to make ourselves understood made the effort tiresome.

CHAPTER XII.

AT LAST we reached Fort Bridger, so named for a trader who first settled there. Later on it was used as an outpost and relief station for the great rush of Mormons to Salt Lake, and afterwards as a fort of the United States Government. We were told that Fort Bridger was the terminus of the Great American desert, and we fondly hoped to get a supply of fresh vegetables within its borders. But the few potatoes were held at such a price that we could not afford to buy them, and they proved to be the only vegetable we found cultivated until we reached Salt Lake City.

As soon as we arrived at Fort Bridger James went immediately to buy some fresh meat and vegetables, never dreaming for a moment that there would be any difficulty in getting them. On approaching the sutler of the fort he was informed that the government did not allow the sale of meat or other provisions to outside parties. No persuasion was of any avail. James tried to explain that his wife was not well and needed fresh meat sorely, but the man turned a deaf ear to all his entreaties. Very much disappointed James turned to go without it, when a private soldier who overheard the conversation said, "Stay, pilgrim, no sick woman shall go without a bite of fresh meat while I'm around. We can't sell any, but I can give her my ration and not go hungry either." In this manner was the meat procured. In return for the kind thoughtfulness of the soldier I sent to him my beloved Ivanhoe.

Most of our journey between Denver and Salt Lake, when not desert, was through and over the interminable ranges of the Rocky mountains. For many weary days we were continually ascending and descending. We no sooner arrived at the top of one rugged mountain, when as far as the eye could reach, other ranges just as steep loomed up before us, and it seemed an endless time before we struck the long gradual slope or plain and arrived at the summit of these grand old mountains through the South Pass, and thence through Bridger and down Echo canyon, where our shouts and songs reverberated from the mountain side. We followed its little stream until we reached that plain which we knew to be the center of Mormondom. Ever since we had crossed Green river we had been told that we were now in the country of the Mormons, and we had been warned, if we desired their good will, we should be careful in what manner we expressed ourselves about their peculiar institutions to the cattlemen or settler whom we might meet on the road. Especially had we been warned not to admit that we had emigrated from Missouri, as the people of that state had incurred the most bitter hatred of the Mormons. It was the Missourians who had ousted them from their first stronghold in Nauvoo, Illinois, and caused them to take the long perilous journey to this distant land, where they could not only preach but practice their religion without molestation. Fearful tales had been told us of how whole trains emigrating from Missouri were surrounded and captured by Mormons disguised as Indians, the women and children kept in bondage, and the men put to death.

It was at the end of a long, hot summer day. We had been winding down through narrow ravines and over the abominable roads still used by all the heavy merchant teams that bore goods and other provisions to the City of the Saints. Emerging from the hills we came out on the broad plateau that overlooked the valley of the Great Salt Lake. The city was still several miles from us, and although we had two or three hours of daylight before us, we had to curb our desire to enjoy the comforts and luxuries that we had hoped to find within its boundaries. Not until towards noon of the following day did we descend, weary, dusty and browned with over a thousand miles of jolting, fording and camping, into the veritable city that so long had seemed a myth. To us poor emigrants it bore a most delightful aspect. It was regularly and handsomely laid out on a level plain. Little irrigating canals flowed on either side of the streets, whose clear cold waters were led into the orchards and gardens surrounding every home. The houses of that time were generally small, one story buildings of adobe, and every householder had an acre of ground to cultivate around his home. The gardens diffused an air of freshness and coolness that all could appreciate, but none more than the traveler who had just crossed the great desert. At that day the City of Salt Lake boasted of only one business street on which were the post-office and principal stores.

Since leaving Denver we had had no opportunity to get letters, and I did not allow any time to escape after reaching Salt Lake City before going to the post-office. How eagerly I clasped the precious missives to my breast when they were in my possession. I was almost afraid to open them for fear that they might contain sorrowful news. Driving that thought from my mind I hastily read one after the other, and when I had been assured that all were well and happy as I had left them, then more at my leisure did I read over and over every word they contained. Letters from home! What a comforting sound to wanderers like ourselves, cut off from the world and beyond the pale of civilized life.

We camped for several days in the outskirts of the city, and enjoyed to our heart's content the green fruit and fresh vegetables that we were able to buy or trade from the Mormon women. These women thronged into our camp with everything in the way of produce, which they were glad to exchange for any articles the emigrants desired to part with. At that period when every pound of freight had to be brought overland by wagons, the tariff was fabulously high, and if these Mormon women could acquire anything by trading their fruits, vegetables, butter and cheese, they were that much ahead. So here I parted with my comfortable feather bed. Every Mormon who came into camp wanted to buy it. At first I steadily refused to part with it, but finally I was offered an amount which in our pressing need for money I thought it unwise to refuse. So great was the demand for feather beds and pillows that I might have sold it for even a larger sum. Through all the journey I had held on to my three flat irons, but for some time I had ceased to use them, as the clothing we wore required only cleanliness. These flat irons I bartered with a woman for a tub of fresh butter which I hoped would last us through to California. And I exchanged a much battered brass handled shovel and tongs for a pair of cowhide shoes for myself, which in a few days grew rough, red and rusty, although they lasted until the end of the journey. I was only too glad to trade them many articles, which I could dispense with in exchange for their fresh fruit and vegetables, butter, eggs and cheese of which laid in as liberal a supply as would keep for the rest of our trip.

While we camped in the outskirts of the city, we found it necessary to buy hay for our stock. This was brought to us each day by a Mormon woman, the hay tied in a huge bundle and carried on her back and shoulders. This required several trips before a sufficient quantity could be brought in this manner, and when we expressed our surprise that a woman should bear such a burden, she replied morosely "Mormon women are only beasts of burden." A man came into camp one day to sell us some grain. While dickering with my husband over the price and quantity, he kept his eyes fastened on me as I stood preparing our dinner. Suddenly he came over and reached out his hand to shake hands with me. I gazed at him in amazement, and I suppose my countenance showed my surprise. He said, "You do not know me." "No," I replied, "I do not."

"Well," he said, "I know you and you are the daughter of Robert Honeyman," calling my father's name. He then said that he had worked for my father when I was a little girl, and telling me his own name brought to my recollection the time, place and circumstances. I could not deny to him that while we were not Missourians yet we had emigrated from Missouri. I felt somewhat startled and annoyed to meet him in Salt Lake City. However, I assumed a smiling face and said, "O, yes, I now remember you well," and made him welcome to our humble camp. He informed me that he had embraced the Mormon faith, marrying a mother and two daughters, and invited us very cordially to visit him in his home. I replied that, if his wives would care to see me, it would give me great pleasure to accept his invitation.

In the evening he returned bringing his wives to call upon me. They were plain, common-place people on a par with most of the women I had seen there, except that they were Americans, while the majority of the women were foreigners. They insisted that we should dine with them the next day. To gratify my curiosity to see how a Mormon household was conducted, I accepted their kind invitation, and we enjoyed their hospitality exceedingly.

There was no reference to the difference in our opinions, and from all I observed each wife was treated alike. The mother, who was also the third wife, entertained us, while the daughters, who were the first and second wives prepared a very excellent dinner. They seemed perfectly contented with the existing order of things. But many of the Mormon women with whom we conversed, were dissatisfied and unhappy. They worked hard and looked worn and dejected. They performed the most menial labor, many of them working in the fields all day in the broiling sun. But I must say that I never saw a community wherein existed so much industry and thrift, combined with so much ignorance and such implicit faith in their fanatical leaders.

We lingered for several days in Salt Lake City and cleaned house so to speak. That is we unloaded and rearranged our stores, repacked our depleted boxes, aired and cleaned our bedding, which was impossible when we traveled every day, brushed out the accumulated sand and alkali dust, repaired the wagon which the constant wear over the bad roads made necessary, and had our faithful old horse newly shod. We were soon to find that we had overstocked ourselves with fresh fruit and vegetables. We hoped that they might last us at least a month, but had not counted on the hot sun across the Utah desert, which so wilted and shriveled them that they were no longer appetizing and we threw them away. The tub of fresh butter, which looked so hard and firm when stowed away in our wagon, was soon turned by the hot sun of the desert into liquid oil by day, though it hardened a little at night. For a while we used it even in its liquid state, but eventually it became so rancid that it, too, was left by the wayside.

We had been told by fellow travelers before reaching Salt Lake that the Mormons never allowed a young woman to leave their borders, and I must confess to a feeling of trepidation as we drove out of the city of Salt Lake. Even when we were several miles beyond its borders, my fears were not wholly allayed. We had heard rumors of emigrants pursued and overtaken, after they had thought they had gotten safely away. The women and female children were torn from husbands and fathers and taken back to the city to be held as wives to some noted elder of the Church, while the husbands were tortured and killed if they offered the least resistance. But happily I found that I had been harboring unnecessary fears, and in a few days I had acquired my usual serenity.

CHAPTER XIII.

The Deserts—Indescribable Sunsets—Alkau Dust—Chance Acquaintances—The Welcome Sunday Morning Flap-jack—Salt Well—Fish Springs—Willow Springs—The Humboldt River—Graves On The Desert

Leaving Salt Lake City, our road crossed the River Jordan. We did not get a view of the Great Salt Lake as it lay some twenty miles and a good day's travel beyond our direct route. We left the green and fertile land around the near neighborhood of the city, and again came on a desert as barren as the great Sahara. Here we encountered sixty miles of almost pure sand. Seas of water would not have produced verdure on its barren soil. The drought was intense and there was no cultivation or industry of any sort. The scanty vegetation was the everlasting sage brush and grease wood which I am tired of mentioning. The mountains and plains seemed to divide the ground equally. The valleys were from ten to fifteen miles across, though in the clear air of Utah they seemed only half that distance. I remember clearly the beautiful sunsets. In this rainless climate the mountains in the full sunlight took on the hues of ruby and carnelian, and at sunset and twilight assumed tints of opal and amethyst. No artist, however skillfully he might handle his brush, could do justice to the brilliant stretches of rare and roseate colorings of these indescribable sunrises and sunsets.

But the arid soil produced little food for our stock. Here and there grew the bunch grass on which depended the life and sustenance of our cattle. Only at rare intervals would we reach a stream whose banks afforded forage for our stock and rest and refreshment for weary and thirsty travelers. Springs were most infrequent and often we had to dig to a considerable depth in the shallow, dry bed of the streams for water, finding barely enough to partially slack the thirst of our cattle. And Oh, the suffering from the scorching, burning alkali dust. It filled the air, penetrated through everything, covered our bodies, found its dusty way into our food boxes, bedding, and clothing. All the water we drank was tainted with its soapy flavor. It choked up the pores of our skin, eating its way into the nostrils and lips. Our faces were continually cracked and sore from its action. Dreary and monotonous as this country seems now as you travel over it in a comfortable Pullman, it was indescribably more so in the days of the slow-moving ox team. It was over six hundred miles from Salt Lake to the base of the Sierras, but the roundabout way that sometimes we had to travel in order to find food and water for our stock made the distance much longer. The best time we could possibly make would not average over a hundred miles a week. At that period for miles over these inhospitable plains there was not a habitation visible. Now on the line of the railways thriving towns and villages abound and the iron horse bellows forth his deep-throated song almost hourly. The thousands speeding over this unfriendly soil little realize the discomforts impeding our slow journey.

We occasionally met some strange characters while traveling on the plains and through the mountains of Utah and Nevada, — men who had drifted over these tract less wilds, isolating themselves from the companionship of their kind, and becoming partial savages. The monotony of our journey was sometimes dispelled by one of these men dropping into our camp, and we became much interested in the strange stories of their wonderful adventures. It appeared that every hour in their roving lives had its dangers and hair-breadth escapes. Some were trappers and scouts, others stockmen and herdsmen. Many apparently had no other desire than to live close to nature and remote from civilization. We encouraged them to tell of the remarkable episodes of their venturesome lives, and it seemed to give them as much pleasure to relate as it did us to sit alternately thrilling or trembling at the wonderful stories. None of the many tales we had read of Western adventure could so have moved us, not even the famous Fennimore Cooper, over whose stories we had burned the midnight oil. Two of these frontiersmen met us on the road one day. They had been alone in the wilderness for weeks, hunting and prospecting. They turned back and went on with us for the balance of the day. We were informed that one of these men was the greatest Indian exterminator on the frontier. His whole family had been massacred by the Indians and his greatest pleasure was in shooting Indians whenever opportunity offered.

We looked forward to Saturday night in camp as a welcome rest and relaxation. Six days' travel was enough for man and beast. We needed the quiet and repose of Sunday. It was not always a complete rest for me, for there was the usual laundering and baking. Still it was a change from the continual moving on. It also gave us the opportunity to indulge in two extra hours of sleep in the morning which proved a blessing to me. Early rising was my "bete noir." The extra time gave me a chance to cook a better Sunday morning breakfast. A yearning filled our souls, or rather our stomachs, for a broiled chicken, fried oysters, or an omelette. Hot rolls we had always for breakfast, but Sunday morning's flap-jacks were our greatest treat. These were made from the sour milk I had carefully saved a day or two. Our milk supply was gradually failing as our little cow could no longer give us a sufficient quantity on the dry and scanty grazing. In place of butter the ever-ready bacon gravy thickened with flour and milk was used. We had both become adept in tossing the flap-jacks up into the air, turning them over and back into the frying pan, and these had to satisfy us in lieu of all the good things that we had in our imagination. We were happy if we had decent water to make our coffee palatable. Travelers on these desert wastes found scant provision for sensitive stomachs. Fortunately our out-door life and exercise found us with appetites whetted for bacon and beans.

By this time my condition became apparent to the most casual observer. Frequently the squaws approached me and patting me on the bosom, would say, "By and by papoose." The urgent need of some new maternity gowns appealed to me every day. But where was I to procure them, hundreds of miles from any dry goods emporium? Necessity, that stern mother of invention, came to ray aid. Before starting on our journey, I had made, to protect it from the dust of travel, a stout covering of blue plaid gingham for my feather bed. This outer covering I had removed when I sold the bed in Salt Lake. Ripping open the plain straight seams, I cut and fashioned without guide or pattern a comfortable and serviceable, if not a stylish, garment, making it by hand at odd moments in camp or as I rode along on my way. From a big flowered dressing gown that my husband had discarded as being too effeminate to be worn on the plains, changing its lines from its too masculine contour, I made another suitable and befitting dress, although the coloring was almost too bright and gay for that style of garment.

Time hung heavily on our hands as we plodded along over the barren stretches of Utah. We became almost as lifeless as the country over which we were traveling. Even by day there was an all-pervading silence. No chirp of bird, no hum of insect. Far ahead of us a white line marked our road. It seemed to ever beckon us on over more arid stretches of desert, sand and sage brush. This part of our journey was one perpetual search for water, and when we were fortunate enough to find it we did nothing but condemn and criticize it all night, grumbling at its quality and lack of quantity. Yet we left it in the morning with fear that we might not again find any so good. The nights were unbearable with the unutterable stillness. The unbroken silence seemed to overpower us with its subdued indifference. It struck a chill to our hearts, and we sought our lowly beds with dread, and timidly slept under the distant and unfamiliar stars.

Just before reaching Fish springs, we passed one of the salt wells that were common to this part of the country. Its depth was unknown, but the water contained therein was so strongly impregnated with salt that it was like a strong brine. This well was six or eight feet in diameter, and all around it the vegetation was covered with a white incrustation. The suction of this strange well was so great that it would draw in anything used in attempting to explore its depths. A rude fence had been thrown around it to guard the unwary traveler.

Fish springs was a large pool of water lying at the base of a low mountain. For three or four miles it sent out a large and copious stream, but the thirsty sands soon absorbed it. The water, while brackish, was said to abound in fish. We threw in our line and tried to coax a bite from the finny denizens, but the only bite we got was from the swarming mosquitoes, immense in size and venomous as starved creatures. They stung our cattle to the verge of madness, and at early dawn we were glad to get beyond their onslaughts. A rude stage station was established at Fish springs, and the solitary keeper greeted us warmly. The sight of travelers to pass the night brought some variety into his isolated life, which had no companionship save the horses and his dogs and cats. We filled his heart with gratitude by leaving with him some of our tattered and torn literature. From this man we learned that the nearest water to be found was over thirty miles away, and he urged us if possible to make the drive in one day.

Next morning, long before the sun was up, we were traveling our way through a dusty, sandy pass. The sky was overcast with heavy leaden clouds. The heat was intense. Peal after peal of thunder shook the air, but only a slight shower overtook us. However we hailed it with delight, for while there was more thunder than shower, we were gratified for any moisture. This unusual rain served to cool the air, and we hurried along with renewed zeal, hoping to reach by nightfall, the point already described to us as Pleasant valley. Darkness overtook us long before we reached its precious locality. We knew, however, that it could not be far off by the way our thirsty cattle snuffed the air, and by their increased gait, which required no urging. A little later we drove into the valley, where the pure and sparkling water of Willow springs greeted us with its refreshing coolness. How we reveled in its pure, sweet depths. Our thirsty cattle drank again and again, stopped to graze a while, then returned to dip their brown muzzles into its leaping waters. The vegetation around Willow springs was the most luxurious we had seen since we left Salt Lake, and as we had overdriven our stock, we stayed there for two or three days.

We were told by the keeper of this station that we were now over the Utah desert, that is the northeast corner of it, though it extended some two or three hundred miles south of us. For a time after leaving Pleasant valley, our road lay over the mountains of Utah, which brought us some relief from the everlasting sage brush and sand of the desert. These mountains were fairly wooded. A few cedars raised their gnarled and stunted bodies from the ground to a height of ten or fifteen feet. There were also pine of equally scrubby character. But in the canyons grew large balsam firs. My little son engaged himself in gathering large quantities of the gum that exuded from these trees. The flavoring and chewing qualities very much resembled that of the spruce gum of the East.

Our route through these Utah mountains led us over innumerable ranges. We seldom lacked for water there, but the way was devious and wild. One afternoon, leaving the higher ranges behind us, we struck a level plain, and saw ahead of us a drove of five or six hundred cattle which their drivers were urging over a low, marshy piece of ground over which had been built a rough pole bridge. Such a large number crossing at one time had torn the frail structure to pieces. As the ground was too miry and uncertain for us to attempt the crossing, we were compelled to wait over a day, until James with the help of the herdsman repaired the bridge, over which our timid oxen reluctantly trod. Our horse for a time utterly refused to trust his precious bones on the uncertain structure.

When we arrived at Ruby valley, we were told that we were in Nevada Territory. I looked in vain for the precious stones that I supposed had given name to the little station. On reaching Diamond springs, I found them also lacking in the sparkling gems whose name they bore.

Finally we arrived at the banks of the Humboldt river. I say banks, for most of the way along its course was little else but banks. I had heard tales of the Humboldt since I was a child. I had studied its devious wanderings through sandy deserts in my geography at school. Mythical stories had been repeated by different people we met on our journey, and yet I was wholly unprepared for the sight of that river which appeared such an insignificant stream. In many places there was scarcely enough water to dignify it by the name of a stream, although it was said to be three hundred miles long. In the fullest part that I saw, it was never larger than an ordinary brooklet. Its narrow bottom at intervals produced a coarse grass, but so strongly impregnated with alkali, that no man who had any regard for the life of his stock would allow them to eat it, if there was any alternative. In some places they had to eat or die and many of them did eat and die, as the numerous whitened bones that covered its banks and borders testified. James turned his stock away from it if possible, preferring to let them browse on the bullberry or the buffalo bush, which grew here and there among the willows. Or if it was imperative that they should feed on this coarse grass in lieu of something better, he would take his sickle and cut the grass for them, as by so doing the stock would not get at the roots, which contained much more of the alkali. Along its ugly, sandy borders no tree worthy of the name was seen. But there were innumerable droves of gadflies, mosquitoes, and gnats, countless and bloodthirsty. There was no comfort to be found either night or day along its borders. During the day the heat was intense, and the thick dust permeated the atmosphere. We thought we had driven over many barren lands, but our pathway along the Humboldt discounted anything with which we had come in contact.

Our pilgrimage through these scorching deserts of Nevada was one long to be remembered. Each morning as the blazing sun arose above the horizon, our tired and sunburned eyes looked in vain for some green spot in all that burning sand, and as we slowly and wearily plodded along its glowing surface, overcome with heat and consumed with thirst, we suffered almost beyond endurance. Unless one has traveled by our slow method, they can have only the slightest conception of these blistering, waterless wastes. Many emigrants whose stock was in no condition to stand this long continued travel without water, found their stock dying and leaving them with no means of transportation. Often they were compelled to abandon their wagons, pack a few provisions on a single ox or mule, and toil on afoot. The bones of hundreds of cattle lay bleaching in the sun. Graves without number were dug by the wayside. It was pitiful and heart rending to see them in such numbers. Scarcely a day passed that we did not observe the lowly burial place of some poor sufferer, who had at last succumbed to the hardships of this long journey. These rude graves were sometimes covered with a pile of stones. Others bore a headboard on which was rudely cut the name of him who lay beneath. For them no weeping willow sighed a sad requiem nor enfolded their lowly mounds with its tender, swaying branches. No marble shaft praised their deeds or told their fame. No flowers rare and sweet rested on the unconsecrated soil. But the horned toad and lizard glided beneath the growth of scanty weeds. Those lying here were lonely now, deserted by the loved ones whose bleeding hearts had been forced to leave them at rest beneath the bitter soil.

Fortunately at this late day the horrors of this region have been overcome. In numerous instances wells have been dug and water led into the arid desert. Railroads have been built, and in this age of fierce and furious competition men and money have overcome many difficulties. And now a trip Westward to the Pacific Coast in a comfortable car is sought for by all, and considered a delightful and entertaining journey of a few days. Since our long hazardous journey of eighteen hundred and sixty, I have traveled back and forth a number of times over much of the route we slowly toiled over so long ago. It has been a constant source of wonder to me how we were able to endure it.

CHAPTER XIV.

Meeting New Friends—The Pranks Of A Cook
—Leaving The Humboldt For Carson Valley—
Climbing The Sierras

We had been in the Humboldt region only a few days, when one night we drove into a camp of emigrants who had preceded us all the way from Salt Lake. Their teams, which consisted of mules and horses, kept a day or two ahead of us. But owing to the sickness of a valuable horse, they had been delayed on the road. The company consisted of a white-haired, and rugged old patriarch from the State of Michigan, with his aged wife and two daughters, girls near my own age. A son and a nephew, together with three hired men who had charge of the fine horses the old gentleman was driving through to California, completed the company.

Their traveling outfit consisted of a substantial carriage fitted up with every comfort and convenience for the tedious journey, and drawn by four large mules, two huge prairie schooners carrying their camp equipage and tents, and another wagon conveying grain and provisions for the family and horses, The camp wagon held every comfort that could be devised for a family tenting on the plains. An immense cook stove was loaded and unloaded every day, for it required a great amount of cooking to feed so many. A dining table of rough boards, strong hickory bottomed chairs, and any number of minor comforts that were unknown to us with only our single team to carry all our possessions.

The old gentleman whose name was Brookfield, was a grand-looking specimen of a Western farmer. He was stout, rather short, with snow-white hair and beard, and a ruddy countenance beaming with genial good nature, and still vigorous in spite of advancing years. His wife was just the opposite, painfully angular, and inclined to be somewhat shrewish, a perfect paragon of neatness, and just as much a stickler for order and cleanliness on the plains as she doubtless was in her well-ordered home in Michigan. The daughters were comely girls of eighteen and twenty with long, beautiful, naturally curling hair that hung in ringlets to their waists, and which curled so tightly that no amount of pulling could straighten it. These curls were a source of great curiosity to the Indians. Their own hair hung so straight they could not understand the difference, and watched the girls most intently. Sometimes an Indian, more curious than the others, would venture to examine the curls. Drawing one out to its extreme length and releasing it, he would look so surprised to see it quickly renew its original curl. The girls became uneasy at the sensation their hair produced and wore their bonnets whenever the Indians invaded the camp.

The son of Mr. Brookfield was a capable and attractive young man much like the father. The nephew was the cook, and also the wag of the party, witty and quick at repartee, and a great practical joker. His name was Bert Brookfield. He called the old lady Aunt Debby and he truly was a thorn in Aunt Debby's side. For morning, noon and night he was ever racking his brains for some joke to play upon his nervous old aunt. To me it was an amusing sight to watch Bert, as he gaily donned his cook's cap and apron preparatory to cooking what he called "an elaborate coarse dinner." Aunt Debby hovered around to see that he washed his hands before mixing the bread. He now and then pretended to wipe his floured hands on the seat of his pants or his nose on the dish towel, or carelessly caught up the corner of a horse blanket to wipe the dust from the frying pan, much to the disgust of his fastidious aunt, who continually scolded and fretted until the meal was served.

The meeting with this congenial company was a source of great pleasure to us, for after leaving Salt Lake I had not even seen a white woman. James and I had gradually grown silent and taciturn, and had unwittingly partaken of the gloom and somberness of the dreary landscape. We no longer gaily sang or joked as we kept step beside our slow cattle, we were tired and jaded to absolute silence and to passive endurance by the monotony of the desert. This lively company of young people near our own ages brought new life and interest to us two lonely travelers. They were all musical. The girls had well-trained voices and sang sweetly, while the young men played on different instruments that they had brought with them. For the few weeks that we traveled together, the time passed pleasantly and harmoniously. Our camp at night was a season of mirth and good-fellowship. And no matter how long and tiresome was the day's drive, or how many vicissitudes we encountered, we each managed at nightfall to furnish our quota of amusement.

One morning at breakfast we heard Aunt Debby berating Bert because the coffee was not up to the usual standard. He insisted that he had prepared the coffee as usual, only the alkali water gave it a disagreeable flavor. I had finished up my camp work and was spending a few moments in visiting them in their camp. Aunt Debby was looking after Bert, keeping up her usual careful scrutiny over his pots and pans to see they were properly cleansed. I observed Bert taking up the coffee pot, and from its cavernous depths draw out a long and loathsome worm which he held up to Aunt Debby's view. With a cry of horror she made a dash for his curly head. He nimbly eluded her clutches, but did not escape her tongue, lashing. He informed me afterwards that he had dug two or three feet into the banks of the stream for that worm with which to electrify his squeamish aunt and had put it into the pot after the breakfast was over.

Another morning Bert arose from his slumbers, making a great hue and cry over the loss of one of his moccasins, and went limping around the camp with one bare and unshod foot. As I watched him beating up his huge pan of batter for the hot cakes that he cooked every morning, he turned and gave me a sly wink denoting mischief on his part. Our drive for the day was to be one of unusual length. Every one was hurrying his or her work, in order to get an early start before the sun grew so intolerably hot. Aunt Debby was busily engaged in helping Bert stow away his cooking utensils. Her tongue in the meanwhile was running over with his many derelictions, while he drolly parried her sharp thrusts at his lack of order and neatness. Picking up his half-emptied batter bowl, he looked into it a moment with apparent surprise and consternation. Then drawing forth the huge moccasin that he claimed had either been lost or stolen, held it up before the horrified eyes of Aunt Debby, all dripping with the remnants of the batter. These and similar harmless jokes he was constantly playing on the irascible old lady.

The few weeks spent with this company were the most enjoyable part of our journey. While their mules and horses made faster time than our oxen, yet at the end of the day, by driving a little later we managed to camp together. Owing to the lameness of their fine bay stallion, they, too, made shorter drives. But after the animal had almost entirely recovered, Mr. Brookfield was anxious to make up his lost time and get his fine stock into California as soon as possible. He decided to still follow the Humboldt to its sink, and from there to take the road to California, where his final destination was to be Marysville. We had learned that the route by way of Carson valley, led us through more fertile lands with better forage for our cattle, a very important matter to us, though it was a longer and. more indirect route. Very reluctantly we parted company with these good people, promising each other at some future day we should meet in California. But alas for promises, we never saw or heard of them again, although we wrote to them and made enquiries concerning them from people of Marysville. Whether they changed their minds, like ourselves, and never went to their intended destination, we knew not. To this day I have never forgotten their pleasant companionship on the desolate plains of Nevada.

As we turned our faces in the direction of Carson river a feeling of thankfulness took possession of our hearts. We were leaving the alkali soil of the Humboldt desert behind us, and though the Carson river was absorbed by the same desert, yet a glance at even its worst features was enough to convince us that it watered a far more hopeful region. Large cottonwoods dotted the banks, here and there were willow, and the wild rose in full bloom occasionally cropped out on its sandy banks. Still the prevalence of drought was everywhere visible, and long before we reached Carson City we traveled over miles of land doomed to sterility. As we neared the town there appeared to be a great rush of miners and prospectors headed for some new mines opened up in that vicinity. Some of these men were so enthusiastic over the prospect that they urged us to go no further, but to locate in the new mines. Our faces, however, were set for California and we would not be persuaded. This embryo town was so small and scattered that we hardly knew when we entered it. Yet it aspired to be the emporium of the new gold region.

The features of the country had notably changed. From the dry and thirsty sagebrush land we gradually drove into soft meadows, with numberless rivulets flowing down from the Sierras. Owing to the shallowness of their beds they were easily controlled, and had been made to irrigate a large portion of the land. Small farms and gardens occasionally came in view, and for our stock we found the sweetest and most nutritious grass in abundance. The village of Genoa was a most picturesque little spot. It stood on a bench between the mountains and the valley, with rivulets flowing through and around it to give fertility to its soil and fructify its gardens and green fields. I was charmed with its quiet beauty and seclusion, the brightness of its innumerable streams, and the grandeur of the neighboring mountains whose emerald verdure impressed my mind with a vividness which only those who have passed long months on a shadeless desert can fully realize. From Carson to the pretty little village of Genoa was a drive of nearly twenty miles. After a night spent in those charming surroundings we began the ascent of the Sierra Nevadas, the last range of mountains we would have to climb before we viewed the land we had traveled so long and far to see.

There were still two weeks of mountain travel ahead of us, and we proceeded slowly owing in a great measure to my condition. The continual jolting of the wagon over the uneven roadway was exceedingly trying to me, so much so in fact that I finally gave up ridings altogether, taking my slow way up the mountain on foot. Day after day for the next two weeks I trudged slowly and painfully through the red dust of the Sierras, from

Genoa, at the eastern base, to the foothills of California. I had always boasted of my pedestrian powers, but when I surveyed that road winding up and still up, my pride in being a great walker vanished, and like the old bishop who was so fond of worldly comfort, I said, "All, all is vanity except a carriage." I could no longer mount my horse, and only by slow degrees made my way on foot, stopping frequently to rest the weary muscles. Then upward again, every nerve as tense as steel and every faculty alert, I climbed with painful toil.

After leaving Genoa, we wound around the curved border of a narrow roadway excavated on the mountain side, and only a little wider than the wagon's tracks. So frequent and sharp were these curves that the forward yoke of oxen would be out of sight as I followed the wagon. Looking down the precipice on which we were traveling I shuddered at the thought of what might happen if our sturdy cattle made a misstep on the narrow roadway that seemed to hang on the mountain side. My little son had been suffering for several days with a sprained ankle and was compelled to ride, so on his account I was extremely anxious as I watched the wagon lurch around the sharp and narrow curves.

The scenery along these winding roads was magnificent. The tall pines grew straight as arrows and clinging to their sturdy trunks were beautiful variegated yellow and green lichens. The smaller trees of these immense forests were here in richest profusion. Hemlocks, balsam, pines, and fir trees filled up the intervening spaces. The whole forest seemed gay with life and motion. Squirrels frolicked and scampered from tree to tree. The agile and graceful chipmunk darted hither and thither in the low hazel bushes, chattering noisily as he ran, as if scolding us for disturbing him on his own domain, his bright eyes twinkling as they peered up at us from some leafy bough. The blue jay, with his towering crest and noisy discordant call, flew swiftly through the dark foliage of the evergreen trees. Here and there a dusty lupine lifted up its blue-tipped stem, all strangely beautiful when compared with the alkaline deserts over which we had so recently toiled.

This first day's climb into the Sierras was a novel experience to me. These mountains were so different in aspect from the bare bald Rockies. Ever and anon a little spring by the roadside gave the thirsty climbers a chance to quench their thirst. As I plodded slowly up the mountain side, I had ample time to observe all the beauties of its ever changing scenery. Winding around some steep cliff new surprises would burst upon my vision, here a transient view of still more towering summits covered with snow, there a glimpse of a stream flowing between or at the base of some deep and dark ravine. These beautiful mountains which rose like castelated towers astonished me with the immensity of their huge pines attaining heights that seemed wonderful. The enormous cones were often a foot long and the rich, green foliage, like long needles, swayed with the passing breeze. Lying prone by the wayside, and crossing each other at every imaginable angle were hundreds of these monarchs of the forest laid low by the woodman's axe. It seemed a sacrilege to gaze upon them in their prostrate grandeur. On every side were huge stumps at whose bases lay the fallen trunks of the once noble trees. Civilization made roadways a necessity, and these grand old trees were the victims of the march of improvement. The Rocky mountains failed to compare with the Sierra range in the variety and grandeur of this great forest growth.

Bewitched by the beauty of the surroundings I hardly realized that I had grown weary and footsore, until the setting sun began to cast its shadows over the pine-hung slopes of these mountain gorges. Looking down this slope far below us lay the hamlet of Genoa that we had left so early in the morning, still in sight although we had climbed steadily above it all that long September day. Under a huge pine tree we placed our tent, cooked our humble supper, and prepared to sleep our first night in the vastness of the great Sierras, breathing that balmy air balsam-tinctured from the fragrant pines. Through the open door of our little tent, we watched the moon as it shone down upon us through the interlacing boughs. I was too weary to sleep, and traced the movements of the bright and radiant sphere until it passed beyond my vision. At last I must have fallen asleep, for I was awakened long before dawn by the most unearthly shrieks ringing through the forest and coming back again in plaintive echoes from the hills beyond. These fearful wails were caused by a death in a camp of Indians who were located in our near vicinity, but of whose presence we had been totally ignorant.

CHAPTER XV.

WE IMAGINED when we had progressed so near our journey's end that we had bid a final adieu to "Lo, the poor Indian." But we were yet to see a more degraded specimen of the red man than had been our privilege hitherto. Certainly the Indians we met in the Sierra mountains were more degraded and more filthy than any tribe we had met in our wanderings. These Indians migrated from the valleys to the mountains in the fall to harvest the pine nuts growing so plentifully in these forests, and on which depended their food for the winter months. We came upon them frequently everywhere through these mountains. The lazy braves mounted, leading the way unhampered and free, were followed by troops of obedient and slavish squaws on foot, laden with huge baskets in which the harvest of nuts was loaded.

These Indians were inferior in size and stature. The largest brave rarely exceeded in height a little over five feet. They were extremely homely and repulsive, with wide mouths and flat ugly noses. Their hair, black as jet, cut straight over their low foreheads, hung at the back and sides in long, straggling strands. The squaws wore their hair thickly plastered with pitch, and a broad band of pitch was smeared across noses and cheeks. They were horribly filthy and covered with vermin, and their dirty offspring were strapped as usual to a board, and carried on their backs. While this band of Indians was busy harvesting their annual crop of pine nuts, one of the young squaws was taken suddenly ill and died. She was the wife of the chief and great was the commotion among them at her untimely taking off. It was the custom among these Indians, when a death occurred in their tribe, for the superannuated squaws to become professional mourners. They would immediately proceed to stain their already tarred heads and faces with a more ample supply of pitch, and then burst forth into the most dismal wails indeed. The forest and mountains reverberated with their unearthly shrieks for the dead. This weeping and wailing was continued through the long hours of the first night and all the following day until near sunset. It was our privilege to witness the strange funeral ceremonies over the body of this squaw. It was carefully rolled in her soiled red blanket, then a huge pile of dried pine branches was erected, on which was placed her dead body. Her nearest relatives grouped themselves about the funeral pyre, while the others stood around the outside of the circle. For an interval of ten moments or more perfect silence reigned. The loud wailing of the aged squaws had ceased and just as the setting sun was about to sink below the horizon, one of these ancient mourners, an old squaw whose head was literally covered with tar, raised her arms heavenward and gazed long and steadily at the sun as it slowly sank from sight. At intervals she muttered some low incantation, her bronze countenance lit up with a strange intensity. For a short space of time she stood in this position. Then, suddenly with a blood-curdling shriek, she sprang forward and seizing a brand from the camp fire lighted the funeral heap. The flames shot high in the darkened forest. The aged squaws, whose bent bodies rocked to and fro in rhythmic time, renewed their plaintive wailing and all the other Indians of both sexes joined in a pathetic chorus, and chanted a funeral dirge sounding to our listening ears like, "Emaylaya, emaylaya." All swiftly turned their faces toward the setting sun, then back again upon the funeral pyre. It was a strange weird sight to us, that circle of bronzed Indians around the burning corpse. While the song or chant was being sung each one swayed mechanically to the measure of the dirge, but their stolid countenances hid any expression of grief or woe.

For several days before reaching the summit of the Sierras I toiled slowly up and over the narrow winding trails, stopping frequently to rest and catch my breath, on and on and always higher and higher, frequently meeting the mule pack trains carrying freight and merchandise from California over to the deserts of Nevada. These mules were burdened with every variety of merchandise, furniture, flour and freight of all kinds, securely fastened on to huge pack saddles. Around their necks was strung a string of bells which warned teamsters and pedestrians of their approach. These mules never gave the right of way to anyone. In many places the road was so narrow and the mountain so steep above and below us, that I was obliged to squeeze myself as closely to the cliff as possible, hunting if I had time, some place that had been excavated a little deeper in the side of the cliff than usual, and standing there perfectly still until they passed me by. Their burdened sides pressed close against me as they crowded along. It was rather trying to the nerves to have from sixty to a hundred pack-mules rushing past one with scarcely room for one's body.

As we continued to ascend, I found that I could no longer keep up with the team and the slow-moving oxen would out-walk me. In the early part of our journey, I could without effort out-walk them, but not so now. My husband frequently halted the team to wait for me. Oh how glad was I to catch a sight of the waiting wagon in which I could lie down for a brief respite. At last we reached the summit in the early days of October and camped a day and rested in Strawberry valley. The atmosphere at this altitude began to grow shivery at nightfall. A keen, frosty air permeated everywhere. Our camp was in the neighborhood of a lumber, or rather a shake settlement. Four or five young and vigorous men from the New England states had located a timber claim in the heart of these immense pine forests, and were busily employed in getting out lumber and making the shakes that were in demand for building purposes all down through the Sacramento valley. With true California hospitality they visited our camp, and as the nights were cold insisted on our sharing the comforts of their cabin for the night. James turned to me to see what I thought of the proposition. I could easily see that he wanted to accept the invitation and have a talk and smoke with these hospitable mountaineers. I, too, longed to be under a roof and sit by a warm fireside. Needless to say we accepted. Before we reached their cabin I heard strains of music from a favorite opera which I was surprised to hear in this mountain wilderness. When the cabin door was opened we found a young man who played the violin with the skill of a virtuoso.

The bright light from within the cabin showed us a most cheerful interior. There was an immense room with a roughly boarded floor. The spaces between the logs of which the cabin was built were unchinked and let in volumes of fresh mountain ozone. In a rough stone fire-place huge logs were burning. A square home-made pine table occupied the center of the room. It held a few books, interspersed with pipes and tobacco. At one side of this room was a rough couch covered with the skins of wild animals and very comfortable. There was a rocking-chair that one of the men had made, the seat and back formed of skins like the couch. This was immediately whirled in front of the fire for my benefit, and it was a great luxury to be seated once more in a real rocking-chair, as for the last six months I had either sat upon the ground, or on an humble soap box with neither arms nor back for support. Indeed the smallest suggestion of home or home comfort was very grateful. The rough walls of the cabin were decorated with the various trophies of the forest, antlers, skins of wild animals, Indian bows and arrows, and guns of various kinds were stacked in the corners or hung on the rough walls. The huge fire place took nearly one side of this room. Around the other sides were bunks built into the walls which served for beds. The mattresses, made from flour sacks and filled with hay, were fairly comfortable when covered with their grey and blue blankets. They whole interior presented an inviting and homelike look to us belated emigrants, and for a mountain cabin occupied solely by men it was cleaner and more neatly kept than would be expected.

Our little son greatly amused these men with his childish prattle, and continually questioned them about the various trophies decorating the walls of the cabin, demanding the history of each one and the manner of acquisition. His infantile opinions, given without the least reserve and with a seriousness beyond his years, caused many a covert smile and frequently a hearty laugh from them. Such a long time had elapsed since they had seen or conversed with a child that they pronounced it a great treat, and he was handed around from one to another until the Sandman caused his weary eyelids to hang most heavily, and he called loudly for bed. One of the larger bunks was assigned to us for the night. Then the men lit their pipes and stole forth into the night, giving me ample time to undress and get to bed. At early dawn they made themselves just as scarce until my morning toilet was completed. A knock at the door was answered by my husband and there stood one of our hosts with a freshly-scrubbed tin wash basin filled with warm water, and a clean flour sack for a towel, politely apologizing because he could do no better for us. The hearty breakfast was prepared in the rough shed adjoining the cabin and I greatly enjoyed a meal that I had not cooked myself. And I found the biscuit made from sour dough and soda most excellent.

While eating our breakfast the men insisted that we should tarry with them another day. They appeared to take unusually kindly interest in us and complimented my husband on the pluck and energy he had exhibited in so successfully engineering his way across the plains alone and unaided. We were both inspired with hope and confidence, by hearing that such enterprise and courage as we had shown was bound to succeed in a new country. Taking James around part of their claim, they showed him their primitive workshop and told him of different sections of good timber land waiting for some one to pre-empt and open up. They told him also much of their own prospects and the already successful business they had acquired. Finally they wound up the conference of the forenoon with an offer to James to stay and go into the lumber business with them, asking for no money in the transaction. Of course we had our good three yoke of oxen which were very much needed in a logging camp. As a farther inducement for us to stay, they offered to build another cabin near their own for us. A family in their camp would add so much pleasure and company to their isolated lives, particularly as the long winter was approaching.

James felt almost persuaded. Here was a business and a means of living opened to us who were strangers in a strange land with little or no capital except that vested in our traveling outfit. I think were it not for my approaching confinement he would have consented to remain with them.

He finally told them that he would abide by my decision. I was weary enough from my long journey to stay and rest, and under other circumstances would have given the kind and opportune offer a grateful acquiescence. But I was young and inexperienced and dreaded going through my coming ordeal so far from nurse or doctor. I have since learned that pioneer women in a new country can do without the services of either one and fare just as well. We enjoyed our stay with these people and reluctantly bade them farewell, promising them if we found no location or business suited to our wants, that in the coming spring we would return to their cabin among the pines of the Sierras.

As we began the descent of the western slope, the wayside houses grew more frequent and we met numerous vans carrying freight over the mountains into Nevada. Occasionally a fruit wagon appeared, with pears, apples and other fruit from the fertile Sacramento valley. This was the first fruit we had seen since we had left Salt Lake. The huckster kindly consented to sell me two pears for fifty cents and I think the price made them more enjoyable.

While we were descending what was then called the Hangtown grade, we stopped to water our stock at a wayside inn. The proprietor noticing that we were emigrants came out to our wagon and said to my husband, "Stranger, have you got any sugar to spare in your outfit? We're clean out. The freighter who was to bring our groceries from Sacramento is way behind time. There's nary a pound of that sweet stuff in the house, and the women folks are all clamoring for it." Fortunately we were able to oblige him with several pounds, and as it was near dinner time he insisted on our coming into dinner with them. I demurred at making my appearance at dinner, even in a country hotel, as my blue plaid gingham gown was much soiled with the red dust of the road, and I had neither time nor opportunity to make a fresh toilet. But all my excuses were overruled, and we were ushered into the rough dining room. I found the other guests were as unkempt looking as myself. While enjoying the luxury of a meal with fresh meat well cooked, and plenty of vegetables with good mountain butter and cream, I forgot I was not dressed for dinner. Never was there a meal more thoroughly enjoyed. The potatoes were soggy and the saleratus biscuit golden-hued. But Oh! such a welcome change from bacon and beans.

As we continued down the western slope of the Sierras we found besides the towering pine other trees with a strange and beautiful foliage; such a wonderful variety of oaks and the picturesque madrona with its bright and shining leaves. The peculiar bark was very curious to Robert, my little son, who discovered when he cut a branch that the red bark peeled off smooth and clean. The handsome manzanita with its brown berries furnished food to birds and bears and to the roving Indian as well. On the down grades as we more rapidly approached the foot hills we felt that at last our feet were planted on the soil of California, the far-famed land of gold, where we thought to pick up the precious metal by the wayside.

How we searched the dust and rocks as we passed along for traces of the golden ore. We observed ditches running here and there filled with yellow water which in our ignorance we imagined was colored by the particles of gold running through them. Along the ravines and near the brooks were men prospecting and washing the dirt and gravel in a queer arrangement called a rocker, in the hopes of finding what they called pay dirt. Many of the water courses had been deeply and widely cut for miles, bringing the water to miners in their different locations. Little cabins serving to shelter the busy miners dotted the hills which were honeycombed and tunneled in every direction, in the eagerness to find the precious metal. We were greatly interested and enthused as we lingered and talked with some of the more fortunate miners who had struck a rich find of pay dirt in the surface diggings. But the beauty of the surrounding country was much disfigured with all manner of ungainly heaps and ridges. Prospecting perhaps was necessary but it did not tend to beautify the face of nature. Beautiful little natural springs abounded, bright and clear, as crystal; but every rill leading from them was turned to liquid mud by some devastating prospector or gold seeker. California in yielding up her wealth of hoarded gold surrendered much of her charm and beauty.

Near a branch of the American river we saw our first Chinamen. These strange looking men were then a source of wonder to us with their queer habits, style of dress, and their long braided queues hanging down their backs or else tightly wound around their shaven heads, that were covered with a most peculiar hat looking like inverted wash bowls made of straw. In groups of five or six they were digging the dry gravel and washing it with a sort of Hume and wheel arrangement that brought the water down into the rocker. Several times we stopped to listen to the curious intonation of their voices. Once we made enquiries of a group of these strange men about the road we should follow, as we had arrived at a point where it forked in two different directions. But they stupidly looked at us and said, "No sabby."

Getting no information from the Chinamen, fate took us in hand and decided our direction. We took the road that appeared to be the most traveled, and thought we were on our way to Placerville, expecting by nightfall to camp within its outskirts. The sun was getting low and still no town in sight. A prospector carrying his pick and shovel and a bundle of blankets met us in the road. From him we learned that we were miles off our road to Placerville, but on the direct route to the town of Folsom. It had been our intention to drive to Sacramento via Placerville as we had been directed and make that city the terminus of our long pilgrimage. We felt chagrined that we were so far off the road. But the prospector, who seemed to be well-informed about the country, told us that we were even nearer to Sacramento than if we had taken the road to Placerville.

Next day at noon we drew near a thrifty-looking farm house, and finding no place for our stock to graze, as all the land was fenced in, we drove up to the barnyard gate and sought permission of the rancher to drive within his enclosure, and asked him to sell us some hay to feed our stock. To this he readily consented, allowed us to make a fire in his barnyard to boil our coffee, and seemed very accommodating. All the time he was walking around our cattle and appeared to be very much interested in them. They, in spite of their long journey, were in excellent condition, looking sleek and well-kept. James was a careful and prudent driver. He was always solicitous for the welfare of his stock and kept them curried and groomed until their hides shone like satin. The rancher looked them over and over again, pleased at their gentleness and docility. He examined our wagon also, and asked numberless questions in regard to our journey, the length of time we had been on our way, and to what place were we going. Finally he ended his interrogatory conversation with an offer to buy our whole outfit for the sum of four hundred dollars. This offer coming upon us so suddenly caused us both to hesitate for a moment before replying. Noticing our hesitation, he added, "I will give you and your family a week's board in the bargain, and that will give you time to locate yourselves." This almost took our breath away, coming upon us in such an unlooked-for manner. We could not in reason refuse such a satisfactory offer. It was a much larger sum than we had even hoped to get although we had been told that horned cattle were very high at that time in California. Within less than an hour's notice, our trunks and personal belongings were removed and our wagon, oxen, horse, tent and camp equipage were turned over to the rancher. Imagine my consternation when he insisted on our going at once to his house. I had no opportunity or time to make a change in my dress, and attired as I was in my soiled and tattered gown, dusty and dirty from the strain of travel and camp; my husband clad in his worn and begrimed red flannel shirt, his rough corduroys stuffed in his rougher boots; my little son in his worn outing garb, we presented anything but a prepossessing appearance. I dreaded woefully to face the wife who knew nothing of the strangers her husband was ushering thus unceremoniously into her well-ordered household. We met with a more civil reception than I expected, although she looked somewhat askance at our worn garb. We were at once shown into a very plain but clean bed room adjoining the kitchen. My trunks were brought in and I unpacked some clean, fresh garments and after the luxury of a good bath and having removed the red dust of the road we gladly donned the garb of civilized society, and looked and felt fit to be once more within the pale of civilization.

When the bell rang calling us out to supper I was pleased to note the change in the demeanor of our hostess, who gazed upon us with ill-concealed surprise. Such is the power of good clothes, for the unkempt and soiled emigrants had blossomed out into really good-looking people. My husband, although browned by six months' exposure to the sun and wind, was wonderfully improved when shaved and dressed in a "biled" shirt and collar and well fitting clothes. I felt proud of him when I compared him with the somewhat slovenly rancher. As for myself I had worn my shaker sun bonnet so closely and was always so vain of my white hands, never allowing myself to go ungloved save when cooking, that I bore no mark of the emigrant, when I discarded my emigrant garb. My fair-haired little son, Robert, looked exceedingly picturesque in his natty suit of blue. I could easily perceive that we were making a new and more favorable impression.

Our bed room for the night was in such near proximity to the kitchen that I could overhear every word that was spoken there. The next morning I was awakened by a conversation between our hostess and the hired man who had come in with his pail of milk. "Has the boss been buying any emigrant cattle lately," he asked. "Yes," she replied, "He bought out an emigrant family yesterday, and they are to stay a week with us." "Well," replied the man, "There are two dead oxen and one cow laying in the corral."

Nothing was said to us at breakfast about any dead animals. But after breakfast was over James went out to the corral to see for himself, and there lay stretched out dead and cold our beautiful black Jill and Buck, our favorite lead oxen, and our gentle little cow. Each of them had apparently been well and sound the day before. Feeding that last day in the open foothills, they had eaten of the poison parsnip which grew there so profusely. At the time of the sale they had shown no signs of illness, either to us or to the rancher James insisted on returning some of the money that had been paid to him but the man would not take it. He insisted that it was his loss under the circumstances of the trade.

Our hostess the next morning gave us a large airy room up stairs. During the day, the elderly lady, mother of the rancher, said to me, "We have a piano in the parlor that we brought around the horn with us but no one here can play upon it. Perhaps you play?" I replied that before we left the States I had been considered quite a musician, but had had no practice for the last six months. At once I was ushered into the unused parlor and the piano unlocked and divested of its rubber covering, and I reveled once more in the touch of the familiar keys, playing over and over my long neglected music. I soon had an audience from all the household, including the hired man and the Chinaman. My effort seemed to captivate them all, not that it was excellent, but because they were hungry for music. After discovering that I had this accomplishment, nothing was too good for us. Each vied with the other to make our stay delightful and begged of us to remain until the end of the month. But James was anxious to look about for business, and I felt the need of getting settled before my fast approaching confinement.

At the end of the week we left the home of these good people, to whom we became very much attached. We found in the neighboring town of Folsom, and five or six miles from our new-found friends, a little cottage of two or three rooms exceedingly small and primitive, but roomy enough for our needs, larger than we cared to furnish under the circumstances. We had not fully decided where we were going to locate permanently, and only provided ourselves with the bare necessities that we must have for comfort.

At last we were settled down for a rest from our long and perilous journey. How I enjoyed the quiet of this humble little home, the cessation from the continual moving on — my morning's peaceful sleep without having to arise at the first peep of day and get ready to travel onward. And here, after an interval of two short weeks the stork put in his appearance and our babe came to us, the mother of the grandsons for whom I pen these lines.

My dear husband was worried beyond all measure for fear that the long and tiresome journey would prove disastrous for me, but I came bravely through the trying ordeal.

I have now finished my narrative of my six-month journey overland to California. Many things have been omitted owing to forgetfulness, or lack of skill in selecting what to many would have been more interesting. Some things have been included which, perhaps, it would have been wiser to omit. I have tried to relate all faithfully as I remember it. While striving with my refractory memories, I realised that they were sometimes unsatisfactory to myself and probably would be to others, and, while I have forgotten much of the less interesting parts of the journey, yet, in the main I have kept close to the most striking incidents of our long trip. As we congratulated ourselves that all was well that ended well, we could happily say with California's own poet, Joaquin Miller, in his "Pioneer"

> *"That rest, sweet rest is reckoned best,*
> *For we were worn as worn with years.*
> *Two thousand miles of thirst, and tears,*
> *Two thousand miles of bated breath*
> *Two thousand miles of dust and death."*